BASIC AIR FRYER COOKBOOK FOR BEGINNERS:

Healthy, Tasty and Super-Easy Air Fryer Recipes
(With Pictures)

Arthur Green

Table of Contents

INTRODUCTION

Do you ever crave the delicious crunch of fried foods but feel guilty about consuming too much oil? Don't worry; you're not alone in this culinary dilemma. Luckily, the air fryer has come to the rescue, solving the age-old problem of achieving crispy perfection without drowning our favorite dishes in oil. It's a game-changer that has made it possible for home cooks worldwide to enjoy their favorite fried foods without the guilt.

Brief History and Evolution of Air Fryers:

Let's take a step back and explore the fascinating journey of the air fryer. The concept of cooking with hot air isn't entirely new, but the modern air fryer, as we know it, has undergone a remarkable evolution. It all began with a simple question: How can we enjoy the crispy goodness of fried foods without the excess oil and guilt that often accompany them?

In the early 2000s, some brilliant minds in the kitchen appliance industry came up with an answer to this question. They created a device that could replicate the results of deep frying using only a fraction of the oil. And thus, the air fryer was born! This countertop wonder uses rapid air technology to circulate hot air around the food, creating a crispy outer layer while keeping the interior moist and flavorful.

Since then, the air fryer has become a must-have for health-conscious cooks and busy households. It's not just popular for its ability to produce guilt-free fried treats but also for its versatility in cooking a wide range of dishes—from appetizers to desserts.

Benefits of Using Air Fryers for Healthier Cooking:

Now, you might wonder, what makes the air fryer such a game-changer in the kitchen? Let's talk about the benefits that have captivated cooks of all skill levels.

- **Reduced Oil Consumption:** One of the most significant advantages of the air fryer is its ability to crisp up food using minimal oil. Traditional frying methods submerge food in oil, adding unnecessary calories and unhealthy fats. With the air fryer, you can achieve that coveted crunchiness with just a light oil coating, promoting a healthier approach to cooking.
- **Healthier Eating Without Sacrificing Flavour:** We all crave the satisfying crunch of fried foods, but the associated guilt often overshadows the pleasure. The air fryer lets you indulge in your favourite dishes without compromising flavour or texture. Enjoy crispy delights with less oil, making sticking to your health and wellness goals easier.
- **Time-Efficient Cooking:** The air fryer comes to the rescue with its quick preheating and cooking times. No more waiting for oil to reach the right temperature or dealing with lengthy baking times. The air fryer gets you from the kitchen to the table in a fraction of the time.
- **Easy Cleanup:** The air fryer's enclosed cooking chamber minimizes splatter, and many parts are dishwasher safe. It's a win-win—less cleaning up means more time enjoying your culinary creations.

Choosing the Right Air Fryer for Your Needs:

The market is full of air fryer models, each with unique features. It can be overwhelming for beginners. Let's simplify the process with a few key considerations:

1. **Capacity:** Air fryers come in different sizes, typically measured in quarts. Consider the number of people you usually cook for.

A smaller capacity (3-4 quarts) is suitable for individuals or small families, while larger families may benefit from a 5-6 quart or more.

2. **Power and Temperature Control:** Look for an air fryer with adjustable temperature settings and sufficient power (measured in watts). This flexibility allows you to customize cooking conditions based on the recipes you're preparing.

3. **Cooking Functions:** While air frying is the primary function, many models offer additional features like baking, grilling, and roasting. Choose a model that aligns with your cooking preferences.

4. **Ease of Cleaning:** Opt for air fryers with removable and dishwasher-safe components. Cleaning up after cooking should be as convenient as the cooking process itself.

5. **Digital or Manual Controls:** Decide whether you prefer a straightforward manual interface or a digital control panel with preset cooking programs. Digital controls often provide more precision and ease of use.

6. **Brand Reputation and Reviews:** Research brands and read user reviews to ensure reliability and performance. A well-reviewed air fryer from a reputable brand will likely offer a satisfying cooking experience.

Remember, the right air fryer depends on your specific needs and lifestyle. Once you've chosen, it's time to move on to the next step in your air-frying journey.

Essential Accessories and Tools:

While the air fryer is the star of the show, the right accessories can enhance your cooking experience and open up a world of culinary possibilities. Here are some essential accessories and tools to consider:

1. **Silicone or Parchment Paper:** Line your air fryer basket with silicone or parchment paper to prevent sticking and make cleanup even easier.

2. **Grill Pan or Skewers:** Invest in a grill pan or skewers for a smoother experience. Perfect for grilling vegetables, meats, or kebabs, these accessories add versatility to your air fryer.

3. **Oil Sprayer:** Control the amount of oil you use by investing in

an oil sprayer. This allows for a fine mist of oil, ensuring an even coating on your ingredients.

4. **Multi-Layer Rack:** Maximize your air fryer's cooking capacity by adding a multi-layer rack. It's perfect for cooking different foods simultaneously, saving you time and energy.

5. **Tongs and Silicone Tips:** Handling hot and crispy food is easier with a good pair of tongs. Silicone-tipped tongs are ideal for non-stick baskets.

6. **Meat Thermometer:** Achieve perfectly cooked meats by using a meat thermometer. This ensures that your dishes are not only crispy on the outside but also cooked to perfection on the inside.

The right accessories will make your air frying experience more enjoyable and allow you to experiment with various recipes.

Tips for Efficient and Safe Air Frying:

Now that you have your air fryer and accessories ready let's explore some tips to ensure efficient and safe air frying:

- **Preheat the Air Fryer:** Like traditional ovens, preheating your air fryer is essential for optimal cooking. This helps to create a consistent cooking environment, ensuring that your food cooks evenly.
- **Don't Overcrowd the Basket:** While loading up the basket with ingredients might be tempting, overcrowding can hinder proper air circulation, resulting in unevenly cooked food. Leave enough space between items for hot air to circulate.
- **Flip and Shake:** Flip or shake the basket's contents halfway through cooking to achieve uniform crispiness. This ensures that all sides of your food receive equal heat exposure.
- **Brush or Spray Oil Lightly:** While one of the benefits of air frying is using less oil, a light coating can enhance the crispiness and flavour of your dishes. Use an oil brush or sprayer to apply a thin layer.
- **Use Cooking Spray for Sticky Foods:** When cooking items that tend to stick, like cheese or certain batters, a quick spray of cooking oil on the basket or food can prevent sticking.

- **Experiment with Seasonings:** The air fryer is a fantastic tool for creating flavourful dishes. Experiment with different herbs, spices, and marinades to enhance the taste of your favourite recipes.
- **Monitor Cooking Times:** Keep a close eye on your food, especially during the first few uses, to become familiar with your air fryer's cooking times. Adjustments may be needed based on your specific model.
- **Check for Doneness:** Use a meat thermometer to ensure meats are cooked to a safe internal temperature. This is particularly important for poultry and larger cuts of meat.
- **Safety First:** Always place the air fryer on a flat, stable surface to prevent accidents. Follow safety guidelines provided by the manufacturer to ensure a secure cooking environment.
- **Keep It Ventilated:** Place the air fryer in a well-ventilated area to allow proper air circulation. This helps prevent overheating and ensures optimal performance.

By incorporating these tips into your air frying routine, you'll achieve better cooking results and ensure a safe and enjoyable experience in the kitchen.

In the upcoming chapters, we will explore various recipes catering to different tastes and dietary preferences. Whether you love breakfast, snacks, or hearty meals, there is something for everyone. You will discover creative ways to prepare vegetables, poultry, seafood, meats, and even desserts, all with the magic touch of the air fryer.

Starting with the basics of air frying is an exciting journey into the world of efficient and healthy cooking. Choosing the right air fryer, gathering essential accessories, mastering tips for efficient and safe air frying, and troubleshooting common issues are crucial to ensure a successful and enjoyable air frying experience. Get ready to elevate your cooking game, redefine your approach to healthy eating, and, most importantly, have a blast in the kitchen. So, turn the page and let the air fryer revolution begin!

BREAKFAST RECIPES

Cinnamon Buttered Toasts

INGREDIENTS:

- Non-stick baking spray
- Salted butter – 60 g, softened
- White sugar – 75 g
- Ground cinnamon – 2½ g
- Vanilla extract – 1¼ ml
- Whole-wheat bread slices – 4

Cook time: 5 minutes
Serves: 4

Per Serving:
Calories 262, Carbs 27.4g,
Fat 12.7g, Protein 3.4g

DIRECTIONS:

1. Add the butter, sugar, cinnamon, and vanilla extract in a bowl and mix until smooth.
2. Spread the butter mixture over each bread slice evenly.
3. Grease the "Air Fryer Basket" with baking spray.
4. Select "Air Fry" and then adjust the temperature to 205°C.
5. Set the time for 5 minutes and press "Start" to preheat.
6. After preheating, place the bread slices into the Air Fryer Basket.
7. Press "Start" to begin cooking.
8. After the cooking period is finished, remove the bread slices and serve.

Bagels

DIRECTIONS:

1. In a bowl, blend the flour, baking powder and salt. Add in the yogurt, and with a wooden spoon, mix until well combined. Shape the dough into a ball and place it onto a floured surface.
2. Divide the dough into 8 equal-size portions. Roll each dough portion into an 8-10-inch rope.
3. With your fingers, pinch the edges together to make a bagel.
4. Brush the bagels with beaten egg and sprinkle with bagel seasoning.
5. Grease the "Air Fryer Basket" with baking spray. Select "Air Fry" and adjust the temperature to 175°C.
6. Set the time for 12 minutes and press "Start" to preheat.
7. After preheating, place the bagels into the Air Fryer Basket.
8. Press "Start" to begin cooking.

INGREDIENTS:

- Non-stick baking spray
- Unbleached all-purpose flour – 130 g (plus more for dusting)
- Plain Greek yogurt – 250 g
- Small egg – 1, beaten
- Baking powder – 7 g
- Salt – 2½ g
- Bagel seasoning – 15 g

Cook time: 12 minutes
Serves: 4

Per Serving:
Calories 173, Carbs 30.1g,
Fat g, Protein 7.9g

Croissant Sandwich

INGREDIENTS:

- Non-stick baking spray
- 4 ham slices
- 4 croissants
- 4 cheese slices

Cook time: 3 minutes
Serves: 4

Per Serving:
Calories 447, Carbs 34g,
Fat 24.9g, Protein 20.8g

DIRECTIONS:

1. Cut each croissant in half lengthwise.
2. Arrange 1 ham slice on each open croissant and top with the cheese slices.
3. Place the top back on the croissants and gently press to close.
4. Grease the "Air Fryer Basket" with baking spray.
5. Select "Air Fry" and then adjust the temperature to 175C.
6. Set the time for 3 minutes and press "Start" to preheat.
7. After preheating, place the croissants into the Air Fryer Basket.
8. Press "Start" to begin cooking.
9. While cooking, flip the croissants once halfway through.
10. After the cooking period is finished, remove the croissants and enjoy moderately hot.

Eggs in Avocado Cups

DIRECTIONS:

1. Carefully scoop out some flesh from each avocado half.
2. Crack 1 egg in each avocado half and sprinkle with salt and black pepper.
3. Spray the "Air Fryer Basket" with baking spray.
4. Select "Bake" and then adjust the temperature to 200°C.
5. Set the time for 12 minutes and press "Start" to preheat.
6. After preheating, place the avocado halves into the Air Fryer Basket.
7. Press "Start" to begin cooking.
8. After cooking, remove the avocado halves and place them onto serving plates.
9. Top each half with bacon, and enjoy.

INGREDIENTS:

- Non-stick baking spray
- Avocado – 1, halved and pitted
- Salt and ground black pepper – as required
- Eggs – 2
- Cooked bacon slices – 2, crumbled

Cook time: 12 minutes
Serves: 2

Per Serving:
Calories 300, Carbs 9g,
Fat 26.6g, Protein 9.7g

Sausage & Bacon with Eggs

INGREDIENTS:

- Non-stick baking spray
- Breakfast sausages– 4
- Bacon slices – 4
- Fried eggs – 2
- Cherry tomatoes – 4, halved

Cook time: 8 minutes
Serves: 2

Per Serving:
Calories 274, Carbs 1.2g,
Fat 21.8g, Protein 17.8g

DIRECTIONS:

1. Grease the "Air Fryer Basket" with baking spray.
2. Select "Air Fry" and then adjust the temperature to 190°C.
3. Set the time for 8 minutes and press "Start" to preheat.
4. After preheating, place the sausages and bacon slices into the Air Fryer Basket.
5. Press "Start" to begin cooking.
6. While cooking, flip the sausages and bacon slices once halfway through.
7. After cooking, remove the sausages and bacon slices and transfer them onto serving plates.
8. Place 1 egg and tomatoes onto each plate and enjoy.

Baked Eggs

DIRECTIONS:

1. Grease 4 ramekins with baking spray.
2. Divide the marinara sauce evenly in the bottom of each prepared ramekin and top with capers.
3. Carefully crack 1 egg over marinara sauce into each ramekin and top with cream, followed by the Parmesan cheese. Sprinkle each ramekin with salt and black pepper.
4. Select "Bake" and then adjust the temperature to 205°C.
5. Set the time for 12 minutes and press "Start" to preheat.
6. After preheating, place the ramekins into the Air Fryer Basket. Press "Start" to begin cooking.
7. After cooking, remove the ramekins and enjoy moderately hot.

INGREDIENTS:

- Non-stick baking spray
- Marinara sauce – 225 g
- Capers – 15 g, drained
- Eggs – 4
- Whipping cream – 60 g
- Parmesan cheese – 30 g, shredded
- Salt and ground black pepper – as required

Cook time: 12 minutes
Serves: 4

Per Serving:
Calories 220, Carbs 9.6g, Fat 11.1g, Protein 12.3g

Chicken & Broccoli Quiche

INGREDIENTS:

- Olive oil – 10 ml
- Frozen ready-made pie crust – 1
- Eggs – 3
- Cheddar cheese – 30 g, grated
- Whipping cream – 60 g
- Salt and ground black pepper – as required
- Boiled broccoli – 25 g, chopped
- Cooked chicken – 35 g, chopped

Cook time: 12 minutes
Serves: 8

Per Serving:
Calories 121, Carbs 6.5g,
Fat 8.9g, Protein 3.9g

DIRECTIONS:

1. Lightly grease 2 small pie pans with olive oil. Cut 2 (5-inch) rounds from the pie crust.
2. Arrange 1 pie crust round in each pie pan and gently press in the bottom and sides.
3. Put the eggs, cheese, cream, salt, and black pepper into a bowl and blend to incorporate thoroughly.
4. Pour the egg mixture over the dough base. Top with the broccoli and chicken evenly.
5. Select "Air Fry" and then adjust the temperature to 200ºC.
6. Set the time for 12 minutes and press "Start" to preheat.
7. After preheating, place the pie pans into the Air Fryer Basket. Press "Start" to begin cooking.
8. After cooking, remove the pie pans and set aside for about 5 minutes before serving.

Spinach Omelet

DIRECTIONS:

1. Grease a baking pan with baking spray. Set aside.
2. Sizzle butter into a wok over medium heat and cook the sausages for 7-8 minutes.
3. Put in spinach and cook for about 2 minutes. Take off from heat and set aside to cool slightly.
4. Meanwhile, put the eggs, single cream, garlic salt, salt, and black pepper into a bowl and whisk to incorporate thoroughly. Put in cheese and blend to incorporate.
5. Place the spinach mixture with the egg mixture in the bottom of the baking pan.
6. Select "Bake" and adjust the temperature to 205°C. Set the time for 15 minutes, press "Start" to preheat.
7. After preheating, place the baking pan into the Air Fryer Basket. Press "Start" to begin cooking.

INGREDIENTS:

- Butter – 10 g
- Sausages – 6, cut into small pieces
- Fresh spinach – 60 g, chopped up
- Eggs – 6
- Single cream – 30 g
- Garlic salt – 1 g
- Salt and ground black pepper
- Cheddar cheese – 80 g, shredded

Cook time: 25 minutes
Serves: 4

Per Serving:
Calories 339, Carbs 3.7g,
Fat 27.4g, Protein 19.6g

19

Apple & Walnut Bread

INGREDIENTS:

- Non-stick cooking spray
- All-purpose flour – 130 g
- Baking powder – 3 g
- Baking soda – 1 g
- Ground cinnamon – 1¼ g
- Salt – 1¼ g
- Vegetable oil – 90 ml
- White sugar – 75 g
- Egg – 1
- Vanilla extract – 5 ml
- Apple – 120 g, cored and shredded
- Walnuts – 65 g, chopped

Cook time: 30 minutes
Serves: 6

Per Serving:
Calories 292, Carbs 3g,
Fat 16.2g, Protein 4.5g

DIRECTIONS:

1. Grease an 8x4-inch loaf pan with cooking spray, then dust it with a little flour.
2. Put the flour, baking powder, baking soda, cinnamon, and salt into a bowl and blend to incorporate.
3. Put the oil, sugar, egg, and vanilla extract into another large bowl and whisk to incorporate.
4. Then, add in the flour mixture and mix until just combined
5. Gently blend in the apple and walnuts.
6. Place the mixture into the prepared loaf pan.
7. Select "Air Fry" and then adjust the temperature to 165ºC.

Notes

8. Set the time for 30 minutes and press "Start" to preheat.
9. After preheating, place the loaf pan into the Air Fryer Basket.
10. Press "Start" to begin cooking.
11. After cooking, remove the loaf pan and place it onto a wire rack for 10-15 minutes.
12. Then, remove the bread from the pan and place it onto the wire rack until it is completely cool before slicing.
13. Cut the bread into desired-sized slices and serve

Blueberry Muffins

INGREDIENTS:

- Egg – 1, beaten
- Ripe banana – 1, peeled and mashed
- Flour – 125 g
- Granulated sugar – 25 g
- Baking powder – 2 g
- Coconut oil – 15 g, melted
- Maple syrup – 35 g
- Apple cider vinegar – 5 ml
- Vanilla extract – 5 ml
- Ground cinnamon – 1 pinch
- Fresh blueberries – 75 g
- Non-stick baking spray

Cook time: 12 minutes
Serves: 6

Per Serving:
Calories 223, Carbs 20.1g,
Fat 14.8g, Protein 6.2g

DIRECTIONS:

1. Put the egg and remaining ingredients except for blueberries into a large bowl and blend to incorporate.
2. Gently blend in the blueberries.
3. Grease a 6-cup muffin pan with baking spray.
4. Place the mixture into prepared muffin cups about ¾ full.
5. Select "Bake" and then adjust the temperature to 190°C.
6. Set the time for 12 minutes and press "Start" to preheat.
7. After preheating, place the muffin pan into the Air Fryer Basket.
8. Press "Start" to begin cooking.
9. After cooking, remove the muffin pan and place it onto a wire rack to cool for about 10 minutes.
10. Then, invert the muffins onto the wire rack to cool completely before serving

LUNCH RECIPES

Potato Salad

INGREDIENTS:

- Non-stick baking spray
- Russet potatoes – 4
- Olive oil – 15 ml
- Hard-boiled eggs – 3, peeled and chopped
- Celery stalks – 2, chopped
- Small red onion – 1, chopped
- Dijon mustard – 20 g
- Salt, as required
- Mayonnaise – 40 g

Cook time: 40 minutes
Serves: 6

Per Serving:
Calories 262, Carbs 3.6g,
Fat 26.1g, Protein 7.6g

DIRECTIONS:

1. Grease the "Air Fryer Basket" with baking spray. Select "Air Fry" and adjust the temperature to 200°C.
2. Set the time for 40 minutes and press "Start" to preheat.
3. After preheating, place the potatoes into the Air Fryer Basket. Press "Start" to begin cooking.
4. After cooking, remove the potatoes and transfer the potatoes into a bowl. Set aside to cool.
5. After cooling, peel the potatoes and then chop them.
6. Put the potatoes and remaining ingredients into a salad bowl and gently mix them.
7. Refrigerate to chill before serving.

Cheesy Beef Meatballs

DIRECTIONS:

1. Put beef and remaining ingredients into a large bowl, and with your hands, mix until well combined.
2. Gently shape the mixture into 2-inch balls.
3. Grease a piece of foil with cooking spray, then arrange it in the "Air Fryer Basket".
4. Select "Bake" and adjust the temperature to 190°C. Set the time for 15 minutes, press "Start" to preheat.
5. After preheating, place the meatballs into the Air Fryer Basket. Press "Start" to begin cooking.
6. After cooking, remove the meatballs and enjoy right away alongside the kale.

INGREDIENTS:

- Ground beef – 450 g
- Parmesan cheese – 15 g, grated
- Garlic clove – 1, chopped
- Dried oregano – 2½ g, crushed
- Breadcrumbs – 115 g
- Large egg – 1
- Fresh parsley – 5 g, chopped
- Salt and ground black pepper
- Fresh baby kale – 225 g

Cook time: 15 minutes
Serves: 4

Per Serving:
Calories 310, Carbs 14.6g,
Fat 10.1g, Protein 39.6g

Salmon Burgers

INGREDIENTS:

- Large russet potatoes – 3, peeled and cubed
- Salmon fillet – 1 (150-g)
- Frozen vegetables – 135 g, parboiled and drained
- Salt and ground black pepper – as required
- Olive oil – 60 ml
- Non-stick baking spray
- Egg – 1
- Fresh parsley – 5 g, chopped
- Breadcrumbs – 150 g
- Fresh baby spinach – 180 g

Cook time: 27 minutes
Serves: 6

Per Serving:
Calories 336, Carbs 46.2g,
Fat 12.1g, Protein 12.9g

DIRECTIONS:

1. In a medium saucepan of boiling water, cook the potatoes for about 10 minutes.
2. Drain the potatoes well.
3. Put the potatoes into a bowl, and with a potato masher, mash them.
4. Set aside to cool completely.
5. Grease the "Air Fryer Basket" with baking spray.
6. Select "Air Fry" and then adjust the temperature to 180°C.
7. Set the time for 5 minutes and press "Start" to preheat.
8. After preheating, place the salmon fillet into the Air Fryer Basket.
9. Press "Start" to begin cooking.

10. After cooking, remove the salmon fillet and transfer it into a large bowl.

11. With a fork, flake the salmon.

12. Add the mashed potatoes, egg, vegetables, herbs, salt, and black pepper into the bowl of salmon and blend to incorporate.

13. Make 6 equal-sized patties from the mixture.

14. Coat the patties with breadcrumbs and then drizzle with oil.

15. Grease a piece of foil with cooking spray, then arrange it in the "Air Fryer Basket".

16. Select "Air Fry" and then adjust the temperature to 180°C.

17. Set the time for 12 minutes and press "Start" to preheat.

18. After preheating, place the salmon patties into the Air Fryer Basket.

19. Press "Start" to begin cooking.

20. While cooking, flip the patties once halfway through.

21. After cooking, remove the patties and enjoy right away alongside spinach.

Beans & Veggie Burgers

INGREDIENTS:

- Cooked black beans – 175 g
- Boiled potatoes – 280 g, peeled and mashed
- Fresh spinach – 30 g, chopped
- Fresh mushrooms – 110 g, chopped
- Chile lime seasoning – 10 g
- Non-stick baking spray

Cook time: 22 minutes
Serves: 4

Per Serving:
Calories 113, Carbs 23.1g,
Fat 0.4g, Protein 6g

DIRECTIONS:

1. In a large bowl, add the beans, potatoes, spinach, mushrooms, and seasoning, and with your hands, mix until well combined.
2. Make 4 equal-sized patties from the mixture. Spray the patties with baking spray evenly.
3. Grease the "Air Fryer Basket" with baking spray.
4. Select "Air Fry" and then adjust the temperature to 185°C.
5. Set the time for 22 minutes and press "Start" to preheat.
6. After preheating, place the patties into the Air Fryer Basket. Press "Start" to begin cooking. While cooking, flip the patties once halfway through.
7. After cooking, remove the patties and enjoy right away.

Chicken & Bell Peppers Kabobs

DIRECTIONS:

1. Put the chicken cubes and jerk seasoning into a bowl and blend thoroughly.
2. Cover the bowl and refrigerate overnight.
3. Sprinkle the bell peppers cubes with salt and pepper.
4. Thread the chicken and bell peppers cubes onto greased metal skewers.
5. Grease the "Air Fryer Basket" with baking spray.
6. Select "Air Fry" and adjust the temperature to 190°C. Set the time for 9 minutes, press "Start" to preheat.
7. After preheating, place the skewers into the Air Fryer Basket. Press "Start" to begin cooking.
8. While cooking, flip and coat the kabobs with jerk sauce once halfway through. After cooking, enjoy.

INGREDIENTS:

- Boneless chicken thighs – 6, cut into cubes
- Jerk seasoning – 15 g
- Large sweet peppers – 4, cubed
- Salt and ground black pepper – as required
- Non-stick baking spray
- Jerk sauce – 30 g

Cook time: 9 minutes
Serves: 6

Per Serving:
Calories 269, Carbs 6.8g, Fat 17.2g, Protein 20.8g

Turkey Meatloaf

INGREDIENTS:

- Ground turkey – 450 g
- Fresh kale – 55 g, trimmed, chopped
- Onion – 50 g, chopped
- Canned chopped green chilies –110 g
- Garlic cloves – 2, minced
- Egg – 1, beaten
- Breadcrumbs – 50 g
- Cheddar cheese – 115 g, grated
- Salsa Verde – 65 g
- Fresh coriander – 5 g, chopped
- Red chili powder – 5 g
- Ground cumin – 2½ g
- Salt and ground black

Cook time: 30 minutes
Serves: 6

Per Serving:
Calories 295, Carbs 23g,
Fat 12.7g, Protein 24.8g

DIRECTIONS:

1. Grease a loaf pan with baking spray.
2. Put ground turkey and remaining ingredients into a large bowl, and with your hands, mix until well combined. Place the mixture into the loaf pan.
3. Select "Air Fry" and then adjust the temperature to 200°C.
4. Set the time for 25-30 minutes and press "Start" to preheat.
5. After preheating, place the loaf pan into the Air Fryer Basket. Press "Start" to begin cooking.
6. After cooking, remove the loaf pan and place it onto a wire rack for about 10 minutes. Cut into wedges.

Garlicky Scallops

DIRECTIONS:

1. Place the scallops, butter, thyme, salt, and black pepper in a large bowl and toss to coat well.
2. Grease the "Air Fryer Basket" with baking spray.
3. Select "Air Fry" and then adjust the temperature to 200°C.
4. Set the time for 4 minutes and press "Start" to preheat.
5. After preheating, place the scallops into the Air Fryer Basket.
6. Press "Start" to begin cooking.
7. After cooking, remove the scallops and enjoy right away.

INGREDIENTS:

- Sea scallops – 700 g, cleaned and patted very dry
- Butter – 20 g, melted
- Garlic cloves – 2, minced
- Fresh thyme – 5 g, minced
- Salt and ground black pepper – as required
- Non-stick baking spray

Cook time: 4 minutes
Serves: 6

Per Serving:
Calories 135, Carbs 3g,
Fat 4.7g, Protein 19.1g

Mac n' Cheese

INGREDIENTS:

- Non-stick baking spray
- Sharp cheddar cheese – 225 g, shredded and divided
- Elbow macaroni – 225 g
- Heavy cream – 120 g
- Water – 240 ml
- Dry mustard – 5 g
- Garlic powder – 1¼ g
- Salt – 2½ g
- Powdered black pepper – 2½ g

Cook time: 20 minutes
Serves: 4

Per Serving:
Calories 488, Carbs 45g,
Fat 24.9g, Protein 22.1g

DIRECTIONS:

1. Put 150 g of cheese and remaining ingredients into a baking pan and blend to incorporate.
2. Select "Air Fry" and then adjust the temperature to 190°C.
3. Set the time for 20 minutes and press "Start" to preheat.
4. After preheating, place the baking pan into the Air Fryer Basket.
5. Press "Start" to begin cooking.
6. After 12 minutes of cooking, blend in the remaining cheese.
7. After finishing the cooking, remove the baking pan and enjoy moderately hot.

Tofu in Orange Sauce

DIRECTIONS:

1. Add the tofu, cornstarch, and tamari in a bowl and toss to coat well.
2. Set the tofu aside to marinate for at least 15 minutes.
3. Grease the "Air Fryer Basket" with baking spray.
4. Select "Air Fry" and then adjust the temperature to 200°C.
5. Set the time for 10 minutes and press "Start" to preheat.
6. After preheating, place the tofu cubes into the Air Fryer Basket.
7. Press "Start" to begin cooking.
8. While cooking, flip the tofu cubes once halfway through.
9. Meanwhile, for sauce, add all the ingredients over medium-high heat in a small pan and bring to a boil, stirring continuously.
10. After cooking, remove the tofu cubes and transfer them into a serving bowl.
11. Add the sauce and gently stir to combine.
12. Serve immediately.

INGREDIENTS:

- Ground beef – 450 g
- Parmesan cheese – 15 g, grated
- Garlic clove – 1, chopped
- Dried oregano – 2½ g, crushed
- Breadcrumbs – 115 g
- Large egg – 1
- Fresh parsley – 5 g, chopped
- Salt and ground black pepper
- Fresh baby kale – 225 g

Cook time: 10 minutes
Serves: 4

Per Serving:
Calories 147, Carbs 12.1g,
Fat 6.7g, Protein 12.1g

Buttered Prawns

INGREDIENTS:

- Prawns – 455 g, peeled and deveined
- Garlic clove – 2, minced
- Unsalted butter – 30 g, melted
- Lemon zest – 5 g, grated
- Salt and ground black pepper – as required

Cook time: 6 minutes
Serves: 4

Per Serving:
Calories 189, Carbs 2.4g,
Fat 7.7g, Protein 26g

DIRECTIONS:

1. Put the prawns and remaining ingredients into a bowl and toss to coat well.
2. Set aside at room temperature for about 30 minutes.
3. Arrange the prawn mixture into a baking pan.
4. Select "Bake", adjust the temperature to 235 °C. Set the time for 6 minutes and press "Start" to preheat.
5. After preheating, place the baking pan into the Air Fryer Basket. Press "Start" to begin cooking.
6. After cooking, remove the baking pan and enjoy hot.

APPETIZERS & SIDE DISHES

- BBQ Chicken Wings / 36
- Crispy Coconut Shrimp / 37
- Potato Croquettes / 38
- Cheesy Fries / 40
- Cheesy Broccoli Bites / 41
- Jacket Potatoes / 42
- Sweet and Tangy Mushrooms / 43
- Spicy Butternut Squash / 44
- Garlicky Brussels Sprout / 45
- Cornbread / 46

BBQ Chicken Wings

INGREDIENTS:

- Non-stick baking spray
- Chicken wings – 900 g, cut into drumettes and flats
- BBQ sauce – 150 g
- Salt and ground black pepper

Cook time: 30 minutes
Serves: 4

Per Serving:
Calories 478, Carbs 11.3g,
Fat 16.9g, Protein 65.6g

DIRECTIONS:

1. Grease the "Air Fryer Basket" with baking spray.
2. Select "Air Fry" and then adjust the temperature to 190°C.
3. Set the time for 24 minutes and press "Start" to preheat.
4. After preheating, place the chicken wings into the Air Fryer Basket. Press "Start" to begin cooking.
5. While cooking, flip the chicken wings once halfway through.
6. After 24 minutes of cooking, immediately adjust the temperature to 205°C for 6 minutes.
7. After cooking, remove the chicken wings and place them in a large bowl.
8. Drizzle the wings with BBQ sauce and toss to coat well. Serve immediately.

Crispy Coconut Shrimp

DIRECTIONS:

1. Place the flour, paprika, salt, and white pepper on a shallow plate and blend to incorporate.
2. On a second shallow plate, add the egg whites and beat lightly.
3. Place the breadcrumbs, coconut, and lemon zest on a third shallow plate and blend to incorporate.
4. Coat the shrimp with flour mixture, dip into egg whites, and then coat with the coconut mixture.
5. Grease the "Air Fryer Basket" with baking spray.
6. Select "Bake", adjust the temperature to 200°C. Set the time for 12 minutes and press "Start" to preheat.
7. After preheating, place the shrimp into the Air Fryer Basket. Press "Start" to begin cooking.
8. While cooking, flip the shrimp once halfway through. After cooking, remove the shrimp and enjoy.

INGREDIENTS:

- All-purpose flour – 70 g
- Paprika – 1¼ g
- Salt and ground white pepper
- Egg whites – 2
- Panko breadcrumbs – 115 g
- Unsweetened coconut – 50 g, shredded
- Lemon zest – 2 g, grated finely
- Shrimp – 450 g, peeled and deveined

Cook time: 12 minutes
Serves: 4

Per Serving:
Calories 310, Carbs 18.7g,
Fat 6.9g, Protein 13.2g

Potato Croquettes

INGREDIENTS:

- Medium potatoes – 2, peeled and cubed
- All-purpose flour – 15 g
- Parmesan cheese – 55 g, grated
- Egg yolk – 1
- Fresh chives – 2 g, minced
- Ground nutmeg – 1 pinch
- Salt and ground black pepper – as required
- Eggs – 2
- Breadcrumbs – 75 g
- Vegetable oil – 30 ml
- Non-stick baking spray

Cook time: 37 minutes
Serves: 4

Per Serving:
Calories 283, Carbs 11.5g,
Fat 13.4g, Protein 29.9g

DIRECTIONS:

1. Add potatoes to a pan of boiling water and cook for about 15 minutes.
2. Drain the potatoes well and transfer them into a large bowl.
3. With a potato masher, mash the potatoes and set aside to cool completely.
4. In the same bowl of mashed potatoes, add the flour, Parmesan cheese, egg yolk, chives, nutmeg, salt, and black pepper and blend to incorporate.
5. Make small, equal-sized balls from the mixture.
6. Now, roll each ball into a cylinder shape.
7. In a shallow dish, crack the eggs and beat well.
8. In another dish, mix the breadcrumbs and oil.

Notes

9. Dip the croquettes in egg mixture and then coat with the breadcrumb's mixture.
10. Grease the "Air Fryer Basket" with baking spray.
11. Select "Bake" and then adjust the temperature to 200°C.
12. Set the time for 22 minutes and press "Start" to preheat.
13. After preheating, place the croquettes into the Air Fryer Basket.
14. Press "Start" to begin cooking.
15. While cooking, flip the croquettes once halfway through.
16. After the cooking period is finished, remove the croquettes and enjoy moderately hot.

Cheesy Fries

INGREDIENTS:

- Non-stick baking spray
- Frozen French fries – 455 g
- White cheese curds – 240 g
- Beef gravy – 240 g

Cook time: 20 minutes
Serves: 3

Per Serving:
Calories 442, Carbs 53.8g,
Fat 18.5g, Protein 15.4g

DIRECTIONS:

1. Grease the "Air Fryer Basket" with baking spray.
2. Select "Air Fry" and then adjust the temperature to 190°C.
3. Set the time for 20 minutes and press "Start" to preheat.
4. After preheating, place the French fries into the Air Fryer Basket. Press "Start" to begin cooking.
5. While cooking, shake the basket once halfway through.
6. Meanwhile, heat the gravy according to the package's directions.
7. After cooking, remove the French fries and transfer them onto a platter.
8. Top the fries with cheese curds and drizzle with hot gravy. Serve immediately.

Cheesy Broccoli Bites

DIRECTIONS:

1. Put the broccoli into a food processor and process until finely crumbled.
2. Put the broccoli and remaining ingredients into a large bowl and blend to incorporate.
3. Make small, equal-sized balls from the mixture.
4. Grease the "Air Fryer Basket" with baking spray.
5. Select "Air Fry" and then adjust the temperature to 175°C.
6. Set the time for 12 minutes and press "Start" to preheat.
7. After preheating, place the broccoli balls into the Air Fryer Basket.
8. Press "Start" to begin cooking.
9. After cooking, remove the broccoli balls and enjoy moderately hot.

INGREDIENTS:

- Broccoli florets – 100 g
- Egg – 1, beaten
- Cheddar cheese – 90 g, grated
- Parmesan cheese – 15 g, grated
- Panko breadcrumbs – 110 g
- Salt and freshly ground black pepper – as needed
- Non-stick baking spray

Cook time: 12 minutes
Serves: 5

Per Serving:
Calories 153, Carbs 4g,
Fat 8.2g, Protein 7.1g

Jacket Potatoes

INGREDIENTS:

- Potatoes – 2
- Non-stick baking spray
- Mozzarella cheese – 10 g, shredded
- Sour cream – 45 g
- Unsalted butter – 15 g, softened
- Salt and ground black pepper – as required
- Fresh chives – 2 g, minced

Cook time: 10 minutes
Serves: 2

Per Serving:
Calories 277, Carbs 34.8g,
Fat 12.2g, Protein 8.2g

DIRECTIONS:

1. With a fork, prick the potatoes.
2. Grease the "Air Fryer Basket" with baking spray.
3. Select "Air Fry" and then adjust the temperature to 180°C.
4. Set the time for 15 minutes and press "Start" to preheat.
5. After preheating, place the potatoes into the Air Fryer Basket. Press "Start" to begin cooking.
6. After cooking, remove the potatoes and transfer them onto a platter.
7. Add the mozzarella and remaining ingredients in a bowl and blend to incorporate.
8. Open potatoes from the centre and stuff them with cheese mixture. Serve immediately.

Sweet and Tangy Mushrooms

DIRECTIONS:

1. Grease a baking pan with baking spray.
2. In a bowl, place the soy sauce, honey, vinegar, garlic, and red pepper flakes and blend to incorporate. Set aside.
3. Place the mushroom into the baking pan.
4. Select "Bake" and then adjust the temperature to 175°C.
5. Set the time for 15 minutes and press "Start" to preheat.
6. After preheating, place the baking pan into the Air Fryer Basket.
7. Press "Start" to begin cooking.
8. After 8 minutes of cooking, place the honey mixture in a baking pan and toss to coat well.
9. After cooking, remove the baking pan and enjoy right away.

INGREDIENTS:

- Non-stick baking spray
- Soy sauce – 60 ml
- Maple syrup – 60 g
- Balsamic vinegar – 60 ml
- Garlic cloves – 2, chopped finely
- Red pepper flakes – 2½ g, crushed
- Fresh mushrooms – 500 g, sliced

Cook time: 15 minutes
Serves: 4

Per Serving:
Calories 113, Carbs 24.7g,
Fat 0.2g, Protein 4.4g

Spicy Butternut Squash

INGREDIENTS:

- Medium butternut squash – 1, peeled, seeded and cut into chunks
- Cumin seeds – 10 g
- Garlic powder – 2 g
- Red pepper flakes – 2 g, crushed
- Salt and ground black pepper – as required
- Olive oil – 15 ml
- Non-stick baking spray

Cook time: 10 minutes
Serves: 2

Per Serving:
Calories 191, Carbs 9.4g,
Fat 7g, Protein 3.7g

DIRECTIONS:

1. Mix the squash, spices, salt, pepper, and oil in a bowl.
2. Grease the "Air Fryer Basket" with baking spray.
3. Select "Air Fry" and then adjust the temperature to 190°C.
4. Set the time for 20 minutes and press "Start" to preheat.
5. After preheating, place the squash chunks into the Air Fryer Basket. Press "Start" to begin cooking.
6. While cooking, flip the squash chunks once halfway through.
7. After cooking, remove the squash chunks and enjoy right away.

Garlicky Brussels Sprout

DIRECTIONS:

1. In a bowl, add all the ingredients and toss to coat well.
2. Grease the "Air Fryer Basket" with baking spray.
3. Select "Air Fry" and then adjust the temperature to 200°C.
4. Set the time for 25 minutes and press "Start" to preheat.
5. After preheating, place the Brussels sprouts into the Air Fryer Basket.
6. Press "Start" to begin cooking.
7. While cooking, flip the Brussels sprouts once halfway through.
8. After cooking, remove the Brussels sprouts and enjoy right away.

INGREDIENTS:

- Non-stick baking spray
- Brussels sprouts – 450 g, cut in half
- Olive oil – 30 ml
- Garlic cloves – 2, minced
- Red pepper flakes – 1¼ g, crushed
- Salt and ground black pepper – as required

Cook time: 25 minutes
Serves: 3

Per Serving:
Calories 114, Carbs 8.3g,
Fat 9g, Protein 2.8g

Cornbread

INGREDIENTS:

- Non-stick baking spray
- All-purpose flour – 100 g
- Baking powder – 2 g
- Salt – 1¼ g
- Unsalted butter – 90 g, melted
- Cornmeal – 165 g
- White sugar – 15 g
- Baking soda – 2 g
- Buttermilk – 360 ml
- Large eggs – 2, lightly beaten

Cook time: 10 minutes
Serves: 8

Per Serving:
Calories 217, Carbs 24.9g,
Fat 10.9g, Protein 5.6g

DIRECTIONS:

1. Lightly grease a baking pan with baking spray.
2. Mix the cornmeal, flour, sugar, baking soda, baking powder, and salt in a bowl.
3. Add the buttermilk, butter, and eggs in a separate bowl and blend to incorporate.
4. Then, add in the flour mixture and mix until just combined.
5. Place the flour mixture into the prepared baking pan.
6. Select "Air Fry" and then adjust the temperature to 190°C.
7. Set the time for 25 minutes and press "Start" to preheat.
8. After preheating, place the baking pan into the Air Fryer Basket.
9. Press "Start" to begin cooking.
10. After cooking, remove the baking pan and place onto a wire rack to cool completely before slicing.
11. Cut the bread into desired-sized slices and serve.

FISH & SEAFOOD RECIPES

Buttered Salmon

INGREDIENTS:

- Non-stick baking spray
- Salmon fillets – 4
- Garlic paste – 10 g
- Ginger paste – 10 g
- Salt and ground black pepper – as required
- Butter – 170 g, chopped

Cook time: 30 minutes
Serves: 4

Per Serving:
Calories 355, Carbs 2g,
Fat 29.9g, Protein 19.7g

DIRECTIONS:

1. Coat the salmon fillets with ginger and garlic paste.
2. Then, season the salmon fillets with salt and black pepper.
3. Grease a baking pan with baking spray.
4. Arrange the salmon fillets into the baking pan and top with the butter.
5. Select "Roast" and then adjust the temperature to 190°C.
6. Set the time for 30 minutes and press "Start" to preheat.
7. After preheating, place the baking pan into the Air Fryer Basket
8. Press "Start" to begin cooking. After cooking, remove the salmon fillets and enjoy right away.

Salmon with Green Beans

DIRECTIONS:

1. Add green beans, half of oil, and salt in a large bowl and toss to coat well.
2. Grease the "Air Fryer Basket" with baking spray. Select "Air Fry", adjust the temperature to 190°C.
3. Set the time for 12 minutes and press "Start" to preheat.
4. After preheating, place the green beans into the Air Fryer Basket. Press "Start" to begin cooking.
5. Meanwhile, for salmon, put the garlic, dill, lemon juice, remaining olive oil, and salt into a bowl and blend to incorporate.
6. After 6 minutes of cooking, flip the green beans. Arrange the salmon fillets on top of the green beans.
7. Place the garlic mixture on top of each salmon fillet evenly.
8. After cooking, remove the salmon fillets and green beans and enjoy right away.

INGREDIENTS:

- Non-stick baking spray
- Olive oil – 30 ml, divided
- Fresh dill – 5 g, chopped
- Salmon fillets – 4
- Frozen green beans – 600 g
- Salt – as required
- Garlic cloves – 2, minced
- Fresh lemon juice – 30 ml

Cook time: 12 minutes
Serves: 4

Per Serving:
Calories 330, Carbs 11.3g,
Fat 17.8g, Protein 34g

Seasoned Tilapia

INGREDIENTS:

- Non-stick baking spray
- Lemon pepper seasoning – 2½ g
- Garlic powder – 2½ g
- Onion powder – 2½ g
- Salt and ground black pepper – as required
- Tilapia fillets – 2

Cook time: 12 minutes
Serves: 2

Per Serving:
Calories 148, Carbs 1g,
Fat 1.6g, Protein 32g

DIRECTIONS:

1. Put the lemon pepper seasoning, garlic powder, onion powder, salt, and black pepper in a small bowl.
2. Rub the fish fillets with the seasoning mixture generously.
3. Grease the "Air Fryer Basket" with baking spray.
4. Select "Air Fry" and then adjust the temperature to 190°C.
5. Set the time for 12 minutes and press "Start" to preheat.
6. After preheating, place the fish fillets into the Air Fryer Basket.
7. Press "Start" to begin cooking.
8. After 8 minutes of cooking, flip the fish fillets. After cooking, remove the fish fillets and enjoy right away.

Tangy Halibut

DIRECTIONS:

1. In a large resealable bag, add all the ingredients.
2. Seal the bag and shake well to mix.
3. Refrigerate to marinate for at least 30 minutes.
4. Remove the fish fillets from the bag and shake off the excess marinade.
5. Grease a piece of foil with baking spray, then arrange it in the "Air Fryer Basket".
6. Select "Bake" and then adjust the temperature to 220°C.
7. Set the time for 12 minutes and press "Start" to preheat.
8. After preheating, place the fish fillets into the Air Fryer Basket. Press "Start" to begin cooking.
9. While cooking, flip the fish fillets once halfway through.
10. After cooking, remove the fish fillets and enjoy right away.

INGREDIENTS:

- Non-stick baking spray
- Halibut fillets – 4
- Garlic cloves – 2, minced
- Fresh rosemary – 5 g, minced
- Olive oil – 30 ml
- Red wine vinegar – 30 ml
- Hot sauce – 5 ml

Cook time: 12 minutes
Serves: 4

Per Serving:
Calories 223, Carbs 1g,
Fat 10.4g, Protein 30g

Crispy Cod

INGREDIENTS:

- Cod fillets – 4
- Salt – as required
- All-purpose flour – 30 g
- Eggs – 2
- Panko breadcrumbs– 75 g
- Fresh dill – 2 g, minced
- Lemon zest, grated
- Dry mustard – 2½ g
- Onion powder – 2½ g
- Paprika – 2½ g
- Non-stick baking spray

Cook time: 15 minutes
Serves: 4

Per Serving:
Calories 190, Carbs 5.9g,
Fat 4.3g, Protein 24g

DIRECTIONS:

1. Season the cod fillets with salt generously. Put the flour into a shallow bowl.
2. Crack the eggs into a second bowl and whisk thoroughly.
3. Put the panko, dill, lemon zest, mustard, and spices into a third bowl and blend thoroughly.
4. Coat each cod fillet with the flour, dip into beaten eggs and coat with panko mixture.
5. Grease the "Air Fryer Basket" with baking spray.
6. Select "Air Fry" and then adjust the temperature to 200°C. Set the time for 15 minutes and press "Start" to preheat. After preheating, place the fish fillets into the Air Fryer Basket. Press "Start" to begin cooking.
7. After 8 minutes of cooking, flip the fish fillets. After cooking, remove the fish fillets and enjoy right away.

Sweet & Sour Cod

DIRECTIONS:

1. Put cod fillets and remaining ingredients into a bowl and blend to incorporate.
2. Refrigerator to marinate for around 40-60 minutes.
3. Grease the "Air Fryer Basket" with baking spray. Select "Bake", adjust the temperature to 200°C.
4. Set the time for 12 minutes and press "Start" to preheat.
5. After preheating, place the cod fillets in the Air Fryer Basket. Press "Start" to begin cooking.
6. After cooking, remove the cod fillets and serve.

INGREDIENTS:

- Cod fillets – 4
- Garlic cloves – 2, minced
- Fresh dill – 2 g, minced
- Unsalted butter – 30 g, melted
- Fresh lime juice – 30 ml
- Honey – 5 g
- Sriracha – 2 ml

Cook time: 12 minutes
Serves: 4

Per Serving:
Calories 216, Carbs 1.8g,
Fat 9.1g, Protein 30.2g

Cod with Asparagus

INGREDIENTS:

- Non-stick baking spray
- Cod fillets – 2
- Salt and ground black pepper – as required
- Asparagus spears – 8, trimmed
- Olive oil – 15 ml
- Fresh lemon juice – 20 ml

Cook time: 10 minutes
Serves: 2

Per Serving:
Calories 297, Carbs 5.9g, Fat 15.5g, Protein 36.3g

DIRECTIONS:

1. Season the cod fillets with salt and black pepper.
2. Put the asparagus, salt, black pepper, and oil into a bowl and toss it to coat well.
3. Grease the "Air Fryer Basket" with baking spray.
4. Select "Bake" and then adjust the temperature to 230°C.
5. Set the time for 15 minutes and press "Start" to preheat.
6. After preheating, place the cod fillets and asparagus into the Air Fryer Basket.
7. Press "Start" to begin cooking.
8. After cooking, remove the cod fillets and asparagus and place them onto serving plates.
9. Drizzle with lemon juice and serve immediately.

Pesto Sea Bass

DIRECTIONS:

1. Drizzle the fish fillets with oil and sprinkle with salt.
2. Grease the "Air Fryer Basket" with baking spray.
3. Select "Air Fry" and then adjust the temperature to 150°C.
4. Set the time for 20 minutes and press "Start" to preheat.
5. After preheating, place the fish fillets into the Air Fryer Basket.
6. Press "Start" to begin cooking.
7. While cooking, flip the fish fillets once halfway through.
8. After cooking, remove the fish fillets and place them onto serving plates
9. Top each fillet with the pesto and serve immediately.

INGREDIENTS:

- Sea bass fillets – 4
- Salt – as required
- Olive oil – 20 ml
- Non-stick baking spray
- Pesto – 125 g

Cook time: 20 minutes
Serves: 4

Per Serving:
Calories 380, Carbs 2g,
Fat 25.1g, Protein 36g

Herbed Shrimp

INGREDIENTS:

- Non-stick baking spray
- Salted butter – 60 g, melted
- Fresh lemon juice – 15 ml
- Garlic cloves – 3, minced
- Red pepper flakes – 10 g, crushed
- Shrimp 350 g, peeled and deveined
- Fresh basil – 3 g, chopped
- Chicken broth – 30 ml

Cook time: 7 minutes
Serves: 3

Per Serving:
Calories 327, Carbs 4.2g,
Fat 18.3g, Protein 35.3g

DIRECTIONS:

1. Place butter, lemon juice, garlic, and red pepper flakes in a baking pan and blend to incorporate.
2. Select "Air Fry" and then adjust the temperature to 165°C.
3. Set the time for 7 minutes and press "Start" to preheat.
4. After preheating, place the baking pan into the Air Fryer Basket.
5. Press "Start" to begin cooking.
6. After 2 minutes of cooking, stir in the shrimp, basil, chives and broth.
7. After cooking, remove the baking pan and enjoy right away.

Shrimp with Spinach

DIRECTIONS:

1. Melt butter in a wok on the burner at around medium heat.
2. Cook the garlic for around 30 seconds. Put in spinach and cook for around 1-2 minutes.
3. Put the spinach mixture into a baking pan.
4. Put in shrimp and remaining ingredients and blend to incorporate.
5. Select "Bake", adjust the temperature to 175°C. Set the time for 15 minutes and press "Start" to preheat.
6. After preheating, place the baking pan into the Air Fryer Basket. Press "Start" to begin cooking.
7. While cooking, stir the shrimp mixture once halfway through.
8. After finishing the cooking, remove the baking pan and enjoy immediately.

INGREDIENTS:

- Unsalted butter – 70 g
- Garlic cloves – 3, minced
- Fresh spinach – 450 g, chopped
- Extra-large shrimp – 400 g, peeled and deveined
- Fresh lemon juice – 30 ml
- Fresh parsley – 5 g, minced
- Red pepper flakes – 2½ g
- Salt and ground black pepper

Cook time: 18 minutes
Serves: 4

Per Serving:
Calories 240, Carbs 3.6g,
Fat 13g, Protein 27.6g

POULTRY RECIPES

- Herbed Cornish Hen / 60
- Rosemary Whole Chicken / 61
- Spicy Whole Chicken / 62
- Marinated Chicken Legs / 63
- Crispy Chicken Legs / 64
- Sweet & Spicy Chicken Drumsticks / 65
- Crispy Chicken Drumsticks / 66
- Garlicky Chicken Thighs / 67
- Lemony Chicken Thighs / 68
- Parmesan Chicken Breasts / 69
- Maple Chicken Breasts / 70
- Crispy Chicken Tenders / 71
- Chicken Cordon Bleu / 72
- Simple Turkey Breast / 74
- Herbed & Spiced Turkey Breast / 75
- Zesty Turkey Legs / 76
- Glazed Duck Breasts / 77
- Oats-Crusted Chicken Breast / 78
- Seasoned Chicken Tenders / 80
- Garlicky Duck Legs / 81

Herbed Cornish Hen

INGREDIENTS:

- Olive oil – 60 ml
- Fresh thyme – 2 g, chopped
- Fresh rosemary – 2 g, chopped
- Fresh lemon zest – 2 g, grated finely
- Red pepper flakes – 2½ g, crushed
- Salt and ground black pepper
- Cornish game hen – 1 kg, backbone removed and halved
- Non-stick baking spray

Cook time: 16 minutes
Serves: 4

Per Serving:
Calories 681, Carbs 0.8g,
Fat 57.4g, Protein 38.2g

DIRECTIONS:

1. Add all ingredients except hen portions in a large bowl and blend to incorporate.
2. Add the hen portions and coat with marinade generously. Cover and refrigerator for about 2-24 hours.
3. Place the hen portions into a strainer to drain any liquid. Grease the "Air Fryer Basket" with baking spray.
4. Select "Air Fry" adjust the temperature to 200°C.
5. Set the timer for 16 minutes press "Start" to preheat.
6. After preheating, place the hen portions into the Air Fryer Basket. Press "Start" to begin cooking.
7. After cooking, remove the hen portions and place them onto a cutting board.
8. Cut each portion into 2 pieces and enjoy right away.

Rosemary Whole Chicken

DIRECTIONS:

1. Season the chicken with rosemary, salt, and black pepper.
2. Grease the "Air Fryer Basket" with baking spray.
3. Select "Air Fry" and then adjust the temperature to 195°C.
4. Set the time for 40 minutes and press "Start" to preheat.
5. After preheating, place the chicken into the Air Fryer Basket.
6. Press "Start" to begin cooking.
7. After cooking, remove the chicken and place it on a platter for about 10 minutes.
8. Cut into desired-sized pieces and serve.

INGREDIENTS:

- Whole chicken – 1 (680-g), neck and giblets removed
- Dried rosemary – 10 g, crushed
- Salt and ground black pepper
- Non-stick baking spray

Cook time: 40 minutes
Serves: 3

Per Serving:
Calories 1, Carbs 0g,
Fat 16.8g, Protein 65.6g

Spicy Whole Chicken

INGREDIENTS:

- Unsalted butter – 60 g, softened
- Dried rosemary – 5 g
- Dried thyme – 5 g
- Cajun seasoning – 15 g
- Onion powder – 10 g
- Garlic powder – 10 g
- Paprika – 10 g
- Cayenne pepper – 5 g
- Salt – as required
- Whole chicken – 1, neck and giblets removed

Cook time: 1 hour 10 minutes
Serves: 6

Per Serving:
Calories 434, Carbs 2.5g,
Fat 15g, Protein 66.4g

DIRECTIONS:

1. Add the butter, herbs, spices, and salt in a bowl and blend to incorporate.
2. Rub the chicken generously with the spicy mixture. With kitchen twine, tie off wings and legs.
3. Grease the "Air Fryer Basket" with baking spray.
4. Select "Roast", adjust the temperature to 195°C. Set the time for 70 minutes and press "Start" to preheat.
5. After preheating, place the chicken into the Air Fryer Basket. Press "Start" to begin cooking.
6. After cooking, remove the chicken and place it on a platter for about 10 minutes.

Marinated Chicken Legs

DIRECTIONS:

1. Add the chicken legs, vinegar, garlic, and salt in a bowl and blend to incorporate.
2. Set aside for 15 minutes. Meanwhile, in another bowl, mix the yogurt, spices, salt and black pepper.
3. Add the chicken legs into the bowl and coat generously with the spice mixture.
4. Cover the bowl of chicken and refrigerate for at least 10-12 hours.
5. Grease the "Air Fryer Basket" with baking spray.
6. Select "Air Fry", adjust the temperature to 225°C. Set the time for 20 minutes, press "Start" to preheat.
7. After preheating, place the chicken legs into the Air Fryer Basket. Press "Start" to begin cooking.
8. While cooking, flip the chicken legs once halfway through. After cooking, enjoy right away.

INGREDIENTS:

- Chicken legs – 4
- Balsamic vinegar – 30 ml
- Garlic cloves – 2, minced
- Salt and ground black pepper
- Plain Greek yogurt – 60 g
- Red chili powder – 5 g
- Ground cumin – 5 g
- Ground coriander – 5 g

Cook time: 20 minutes
Serves: 4

Per Serving:
Calories 450, Carbs 2.2g,
Fat 17.2g, Protein 66.7g

Crispy Chicken Legs

INGREDIENTS:

- Chicken legs – 3
- Buttermilk – 240 ml
- White flour – 260 g
- Onion powder – 5 g
- Paprika – 5 g
- Garlic powder – 5 g
- Ground cumin – 5 g
- Salt and ground black pepper
- Olive oil – 15 ml

Cook time: 20 minutes
Serves: 3

Per Serving:
Calories 817, Carbs 69.5g,
Fat 23.3g, Protein 77.4g

DIRECTIONS:

1. Place the chicken legs and buttermilk in a bowl and refrigerate for about 2 hours.
2. In a shallow dish, mix the flour and spices. Remove the chicken from buttermilk.
3. Coat the chicken legs with flour mixture, dip them into buttermilk, and finally, coat them with the flour mixture again. Drizzle the chicken legs with the oil.
4. Grease the "Air Fryer Basket" with baking spray.
5. Select "Air Fry", adjust the temperature to 185°C. Set the time for 20 minutes, press "Start" to preheat.
6. After preheating, place the chicken legs into the Air Fryer Basket. Press "Start" to begin cooking.
7. While cooking, flip the chicken legs once halfway through. After cooking, enjoy right away.

Sweet & Spicy Chicken Drumsticks

DIRECTIONS:

1. For the marinade: in a large bowl, mix garlic, mustard, brown sugar, oil, and spices.
2. Add the chicken drumsticks and coat with marinade generously.
3. Refrigerate to marinate for about 20-30 minutes.
4. Grease the "Air Fryer Basket" with baking spray.
5. Select "Bake", adjust the temperature to 220°C. Set the time for 40 minutes and press "Start" to preheat.
6. After preheating, place the chicken drumstick into the Air Fryer Basket. Press "Start" to begin cooking.
7. After 25 minutes of cooking, flip the drumsticks.
8. After cooking, remove the chicken drumstick and enjoy right away.

INGREDIENTS:

- Vegetable oil – 15 ml
- Garlic clove – 1, crushed
- Mustard – 20 g
- Brown sugar – 10 g
- Red chili powder – 5 g
- Cayenne powder – 5 g
- Salt and ground black pepper
- Chicken drumsticks – 4

Cook time: 40 minutes
Serves: 4

Per Serving:
Calories 341, Carbs 3.3g,
Fat 14.1g, Protein 47.3g

Crispy Chicken Drumsticks

INGREDIENTS:

- Chicken drumsticks – 4
- Buttermilk – 120 ml
- All-purpose flour – 65 g
- Panko breadcrumbs – 75 g
- Baking powder – 1 g
- Dried oregano – 1¼ g
- Dried thyme – 1¼ g
- Garlic powder – 1¼ g
- Celery salt – 1¼ g
- Paprika – 1¼ g
- Cayenne powder – 1¼ g
- Salt and ground black pepper
- Butter – 45 g, melted

Cook time: 20 minutes
Serves: 4

Per Serving:
Calories 388, Carbs 16.1g,
Fat 16.5g, Protein 34.4g

DIRECTIONS:

1. Place the chicken drumsticks and buttermilk in a resealable plastic bag. Refrigerate for about 2-3 hours.
2. Mix the flour, breadcrumbs, baking powder, herbs, and spices in a shallow bowl.
3. Remove the chicken drumsticks from the bag and shake off the excess buttermilk.
4. Coat chicken drumsticks with the seasoned flour mixture evenly.
5. Grease a piece of foil with baking spray, then arrange it in the "Air Fryer Basket".
6. Select "Air Fry", adjust the temperature to 200°C. Set the time for 20 minutes, press "Start" to preheat.
7. After preheating, place the chicken drumsticks into the Air Fryer Basket. Press "Start" to begin cooking.
8. After 10 minutes of cooking, flip the chicken drumsticks and drizzle with melted butter.
9. After cooking, remove the chicken drumsticks and enjoy right away.

Garlicky Chicken Thighs

DIRECTIONS:

1. Rub the chicken thighs evenly with parsley, salt, and black pepper, then brush with melted butter.
2. Grease the "Air Fryer Basket" with baking spray.
3. Select "Bake", adjust the temperature to 235°C. Set the time for 20 minutes and press "Start" to preheat.
4. After preheating, place the chicken thighs into the Air Fryer Basket. Press "Start" to begin cooking.
5. While cooking, flip the chicken thighs once halfway through. After cooking, enjoy right away.

INGREDIENTS:

- Boneless chicken thighs – 4
- Dried parsley – 5 g
- Salt and ground black pepper
- Butter – 30 g, melted

Cook time: 20 minutes
Serves: 4

Per Serving:
Calories 193, Carbs 0g,
Fat 9.8g, Protein 25.4g

Lemony Chicken Thighs

INGREDIENTS:

- Boneless chicken thighs – 6
- Fresh lemon juice – 45 ml
- Dried oregano – 5 g
- Garlic powder – 5 g
- Paprika – 5 g

Cook time: 12 minutes
Serves: 6

Per Serving:
Calories 220, Carbs 0.8g,
Fat 8.5g, Protein 33g

DIRECTIONS:

1. Put chicken thighs and remaining ingredients into a large bowl and blend to incorporate.
2. Refrigerate to marinate for about 30 minutes.
3. Grease the "Air Fryer Basket" with baking spray.
4. Select "Air Fry", adjust the temperature to 200°C. Set the time for 12 minutes and press "Start" to preheat.
5. After preheating, place the chicken thighs into the Air Fryer Basket. Press "Start" to begin cooking.
6. While cooking, flip the chicken thighs once halfway through. After cooking, enjoy right away.

Parmesan Chicken Breasts

DIRECTIONS:

1. In a shallow bowl, mix the breadcrumbs and cheese.
2. Spread mayonnaise evenly on both sides of each chicken breast.
3. Now, coat each chicken breast with the parmesan mixture.
4. Grease the "Air Fryer Basket" with baking spray.
5. Select "Air Fry" and then adjust the temperature to 200ºC.
6. Set the time for 15 minutes and press "Start" to preheat.
7. After preheating, place the chicken breasts into the Air Fryer Basket.
8. Press "Start" to begin cooking.
9. While cooking, flip the chicken breasts once halfway through.
10. After cooking, remove the chicken breasts and enjoy right away.

INGREDIENTS:

- Panko breadcrumbs – 150 g
- Parmesan cheese – 110 g, shredded
- Boneless chicken breasts – 4, pounded slightly
- Mayonnaise – 130 g
- Non-stick baking spray

Cook time: 15 minutes
Serves: 4

Per Serving:
Calories 679, Carbs 18.8g,
Fat 37.5g, Protein 49.8g

Maple Chicken Breasts

INGREDIENTS:

- Boneless chicken breasts – 4
- Fresh lemon juice – 30 ml
- Mustard – 20 g
- Maple syrup – 80 g
- Balsamic vinegar – 60 ml
- Olive oil – 30 ml
- Dried rosemary – 5 g
- Salt and ground black pepper
- Non-stick baking spray

Cook time: 20 minutes
Serves: 4

Per Serving:
Calories 424, Carbs 28.2g,
Fat 17g, Protein 40

DIRECTIONS:

1. Add chicken breasts and remaining ingredients in a large bowl and blend to incorporate.
2. Refrigerate to marinate for at least 2 hours. Grease the "Air Fryer Basket" with baking spray.
3. Select "Bake" and then adjust the temperature to 200°C.
4. Set the time for 20 minutes and press "Start" to preheat.
5. After preheating, place the chicken breasts into the Air Fryer Basket. Press "Start" to begin cooking.
6. While cooking, flip the chicken breasts once halfway through.
7. After cooking, remove the chicken breasts and enjoy right away.

Crispy Chicken Tenders

DIRECTIONS:

1. In a shallow dish, put the flour. In a second shallow dish, place the eggs and whisk lightly.
2. In a third shallow dish, put the breadcrumbs. Rub the chicken tenders with salt.
3. Coat the chicken tenders with flour, dip them into the beaten eggs, and coat them with breadcrumbs.
4. Grease the "Air Fryer Basket" with baking spray.
5. Select "Roast" and then adjust the temperature to 185°C.
6. Set the time for 12 minutes and press "Start" to preheat.
7. After preheating, place the chicken tenders into the Air Fryer Basket. Press "Start" to begin cooking.
8. After cooking, remove the chicken tenders and enjoy right away.

INGREDIENTS:

- All-purpose flour – 110 g
- Eggs – 3, beaten
- Breadcrumbs – 250 g
- Chicken tenderloins – 450 g
- Salt – as required
- Non-stick baking spray

Cook time: 12 minutes
Serves: 4

Per Serving:
Calories 471, Carbs 63g,
Fat 7.1g, Protein 37.5g

Chicken Cordon Bleu

INGREDIENTS:

- Boneless chicken breast halves – 2, pounded slightly
- All-purpose flour – 65 g
- Paprika – 1 g
- Large egg – 1
- Unsalted butter – 15 g, melted
- Ham slices – 2
- Swiss cheese slices – 2
- Salt and ground black pepper
- 2% milk – 30 ml
- Seasoned breadcrumbs – 75 g
- Olive oil – 15 ml

Cook time: 25 minutes
Serves: 2

Per Serving:
Calories 672, Carbs 45.4g,
Fat 28g, Protein 56.2g

DIRECTIONS:

1. Arrange the chicken breast halves onto a smooth surface. Arrange 1 ham slice over each chicken breast half, followed by the cheese. Roll up each chicken breast half and tuck in the ends. With toothpicks, secure the rolls. Mix the flour, paprika, salt, and black pepper on a shallow plate.
2. In a shallow bowl, place the egg and milk and beat slightly. In a second shallow plate, place the breadcrumbs. Coat each chicken roll with flour, dip into egg, and coat with breadcrumbs.
3. Heat the oil over medium heat in a small skillet and cook the chicken rolls for 3-5 minutes.

Notes

4. Remove from heat and set aside. Grease the "Air Fryer Basket" with baking spray.
5. Select "Bake", adjust the temperature to 175°C. Set the time for 25 minutes, press "Start" to preheat.
6. After preheating, place the chicken rolls into the Air Fryer Basket. Press "Start" to begin cooking.
7. After 15 minutes of cooking, flip the chicken rolls. After cooking, remove the rolls and enjoy right away.

Simple Turkey Breast

INGREDIENTS:

- Bone-in, skin-on turkey breast half – 1 (1¼-kg)
- Salt and ground black pepper – as required
- Non-stick baking spray

Cook time: 1 hour 20 minutes
Serves: 6

Per Serving:
Calories 221, Carbs 0g,
Fat 0.8g, Protein 51.6g

DIRECTIONS:

1. Rub the turkey breast with the salt and black pepper evenly.
2. Grease the "Air Fryer Basket" with baking spray.
3. Select "Roast" and then adjust the temperature to 230°C.
4. Set the time for 80 minutes and press "Start" to preheat.
5. After preheating, place the turkey breast into the Air Fryer Basket.
6. Press "Start" to begin cooking.
7. After cooking, remove the turkey breast and place it onto a cutting board.
8. Cover the turkey breast for about 20 minutes with a piece of foil.
9. Cut the turkey breast into desired-size slices and serve.

Herbed & Spiced Turkey Breast

DIRECTIONS:

1. Add the butter, herbs, salt, and black pepper in a bowl and blend to incorporate.
2. Rub the herb mixture under the skin evenly. Coat the outside of the turkey breast with oil.
3. Grease the "Air Fryer Basket" with baking spray. Select "Bake" and then adjust the temperature to 175°C.
4. Set the time for 50 minutes and press "Start" to preheat.
5. After preheating, place the turkey breast into the Air Fryer Basket. Press "Start" to begin cooking.
6. While cooking, flip the turkey breast once halfway through.
7. After cooking, remove the turkey breast and place it onto a cutting board.
8. Cover the turkey breast for about 20 minutes with a piece of foil.
9. Cut the turkey breast into desired-size slices and serve.

INGREDIENTS:

- Unsalted butter – 60 g, softened
- Fresh rosemary – 2 g, chopped
- Fresh thyme – 2 g, chopped
- Fresh sage – 2 g, chopped
- Fresh parsley – 2 g, chopped
- Salt and ground black pepper
- Bone-in, skin-on turkey breast – 1 (1820-g)
- Olive oil – 30 ml
- Non-stick baking spray

Cook time: 50 minutes
Serves: 6

Per Serving:
Calories 333, Carbs 1.8g, Fat 37g, Protein 65.1g

Zesty Turkey Legs

INGREDIENTS:

- Garlic cloves – 2, minced
- Fresh rosemary – 2 g, minced
- Lime zest – 2 g, finely grated
- Olive oil – 30 ml
- Fresh lime juice – 15 ml
- Salt and ground black pepper
- Turkey legs – 2
- Non-stick baking spray

Cook time: 30 minutes
Serves: 2

Per Serving:
Calories 709, Carbs 2.3g,
Fat 32.7g, Protein 97.2g

DIRECTIONS:

1. Mix the garlic, rosemary, lime zest, oil, lime juice, salt, and black pepper in a large bowl.
2. Add the turkey legs and generously coat with marinade. Refrigerate to marinate for about 6-8 hours.
3. Grease the "Air Fryer Basket" with baking spray. Select "Air Fry", adjust the temperature to 175°C.
4. Set the time for 30 minutes and press "Start" to preheat.
5. After preheating, place the turkey legs into the Air Fryer Basket. Press "Start" to begin cooking.
6. While cooking, flip the turkey legs once halfway through. After cooking, enjoy right away.

Glazed Duck Breasts

DIRECTIONS:

1. Grease the "Air Fryer Basket" with baking spray. Select "Air Fry", adjust the temperature to 185°C.
2. Set the time for 20 minutes and press "Start" to preheat.
3. After preheating, place the duck breast into the Air Fryer Basket. Press "Start" to begin cooking.
4. Meanwhile, in a bowl, mix the remaining ingredients.
5. After 15 minutes of cooking, coat the duck breast generously with the honey mixture.
6. After cooking, remove the duck breast and place it onto a cutting board.
7. Cut the duck breast into desired-size slices and serve.

INGREDIENTS:

- Non-stick baking spray
- Duck breast – 1
- Wholegrain mustard – 20 g
- Honey – 5 g
- Balsamic vinegar 5 ml
- Salt and ground black pepper – as required

Cook time: 20 minutes
Serves: 1

Per Serving:
Calories 229, Carbs 4.9g,
Fat 7.6g, Protein 34.2g

Oats-Crusted Chicken Breast

INGREDIENTS:

- Boneless chicken breasts – 2
- Salt and ground black pepper
- Oats – 75 g
- Mustard powder – 30 g
- Fresh parsley – 2 g
- Eggs – 2
- Non-stick baking spray

Cook time: 12 minutes
Serves: 2

Per Serving:
Calories 249, Carbs 17g,
Fat 8.6g, Protein 26g

DIRECTIONS:

1. Place the chicken breasts onto a cutting board and flatten each with a meat mallet into even thicknesses.
2. Then, cut each breast in half. Sprinkle the chicken pieces with salt and black pepper and set aside.
3. Add the oats, mustard powder, parsley, salt, and black pepper in a blender and process to form a coarse breadcrumb-like mixture. Transfer the oat mixture into a shallow bowl.
4. In another bowl, crack the eggs and beat well.
5. Coat the chicken pieces with the oat mixture, dip into beaten eggs, and coat with the oats mixture again.

Notes

6. Grease the "Air Fryer Basket" with baking spray.
7. Select "Air Fry", adjust the temperature to 175°C. Set the time for 12 minutes and press "Start" to preheat.
8. After preheating, place the chicken pieces into the Air Fryer Basket. Press "Start" to begin cooking.
9. While cooking, flip the chicken pieces once halfway through. After cooking, enjoy right away.

Seasoned Chicken Tenders

INGREDIENTS:

- Chicken tenders – 250 g
- BBQ seasoning – 5 g
- Salt and ground black pepper – as required
- Non-stick baking spray

Cook time: 10 minutes
Serves: 2

Per Serving:
Calories 220, Carbs 0.5g,
Fat 8.4g, Protein 32.8g

DIRECTIONS:

1. Season the chicken tenders with BBQ seasoning, salt, and black pepper.
2. Grease the "Air Fryer Basket" with baking spray. Select "Bake" and then adjust the temperature to 235°C.
3. Set the time for 10 minutes and press "Start" to preheat.
4. After preheating, place the chicken tenders into the Air Fryer Basket. Press "Start" to begin cooking.
5. While cooking, flip the chicken tenders once halfway through. After cooking, enjoy right away.

Garlicky Duck Legs

DIRECTIONS:

1. Mix the garlic, parsley, five-spice powder, salt and black pepper in a bowl.
2. Rub the duck legs with the garlic mixture generously.
3. Grease the "Air Fryer Basket" with baking spray.
4. Select "Roast" and then adjust the temperature to 200°C.
5. Set the time for 25 minutes and press "Start" to preheat.
6. After preheating, place the duck legs into the Air Fryer Basket.
7. Press "Start" to begin cooking.
8. After 25 minutes of cooking, adjust the temperature to 220 °C for 10 minutes.
9. After cooking, remove the duck legs and enjoy right away.

INGREDIENTS:

- Non-stick baking spray
- Garlic cloves – 2, minced
- Fresh parsley – 2 g, chopped
- Five spice powder – 5 g
- Salt and ground black pepper – as required
- Duck legs – 2

Cook time: 35 minutes
Serves: 2

Per Serving:
Calories 434, Carbs 1.1g,
Fat 14.4g, Protein 70.4g

MEAT RECIPES

- Buttered Filet Mignon / 84
- Spiced Flank Steak / 85
- Buttered Rib-Eye Steak / 86
- Spiced Beef Sirloin Roast / 87
- Herbed Beef Chuck Roast / 88
- Glazed Beef Short Ribs / 89
- Crispy Sirloin Steaks / 90
- Beef Casserole / 91
- BBQ Pork Chops / 92
- Spiced Pork Chops / 93
- Rosemary Pork Loin / 94
- Caramelized Pork Shoulder / 95
- BBQ Pork Ribs / 96
- Seasoned Pork Tenderloin / 97
- Stuffed Pork Roll / 98
- Garlicky Lamb Chops / 99
- Sweet & Sour Lamb Chops / 100
- Almond Crusted Rack of Lamb / 101
- Rosemary Leg of Lamb / 102
- Pork with Sweet Pepper / 103

Buttered Filet Mignon

INGREDIENTS:

- Filet mignon – 2
- Butter – 15 g, softened
- Salt and ground black pepper – as required
- Non-stick baking spray

DIRECTIONS:

1. Coat both sides of the filet with butter and then season with salt and black pepper.
2. Grease the "Air Fryer Basket" with baking spray. Select "Air Fry" and adjust the temperature to 200°C.
3. Set the time for 14 minutes and press "Start" to preheat.
4. After preheating, place the filets into the Air Fryer Basket. Press "Start" to begin cooking.
5. While cooking, flip the filets once halfway through. After cooking, remove the filets and enjoy right away.

Cook time: 14 minutes
Serves: 2

Per Serving:
Calories 355, Carbs 0g,
Fat 17g, Protein 47.8g

Spiced Flank Steak

DIRECTIONS:

1. Mix the vinegar, spices, salt, and black pepper in a large bowl.
2. Add the steak and coat with mixture generously.
3. Cover the bowl and place in the refrigerator for at least 1 hour.
4. Grease the "Air Fryer Basket" with baking spray.
5. Select "Bake" and then adjust the temperature to 220°C.
6. Set the time for 18 minutes and press "Start" to preheat.
7. After preheating, place the steak into the Air Fryer Basket. Press "Start" to begin cooking.
8. While cooking, flip the steak once halfway through.
9. After cooking, remove the steak and place it onto a cutting board.
10. Cut the steak into desired-sized slices and serve.

INGREDIENTS:

- Balsamic vinegar – 30 ml
- Olive oil – 30 ml
- Garlic cloves – 3, minced
- Red chili powder – 5 g
- Ground cumin – 5 g
- Onion powder – 5 g
- Salt and ground black pepper
- Flank steak – 1
- Non-stick baking spray

Cook time: 18 minutes
Serves: 6

Per Serving:
Calories 341, Carbs 1.3g,
Fat 17.4g, Protein 42.3g

Buttered Rib-Eye Steak

INGREDIENTS:

- Rib-eye steaks – 2
- Unsalted butter – 30 g, melted
- Salt and ground black pepper – as required
- Non-stick baking spray

Cook time: 14 minutes
Serves: 2

Per Serving:
Calories 388, Carbs 0g,
Fat 23.7g, Protein 41g

DIRECTIONS:

1. Coat the steak with butter and sprinkle with salt and black pepper evenly.
2. Grease the "Air Fryer Basket" with baking spray. Select "Roast" and adjust the temperature to 200°C.
3. Set the time for 14 minutes and press "Start" to preheat.
4. After preheating, place the steaks into the Air Fryer Basket. Press "Start" to begin cooking.
5. While cooking, flip the steaks once halfway through.
6. After cooking, remove the steaks and place them onto a platter for about 5 minutes.
7. Cut each steak into desired size slices and serve.

Spiced Beef Sirloin Roast

DIRECTIONS:

1. In a bowl, mix the spices, salt and black pepper.
2. Rub the roast with the spice mixture generously.
3. Grease the "Air Fryer Basket" with baking spray.
4. Select "Roast" and then adjust the temperature to 175°C.
5. Set the time for 50 minutes and press "Start" to preheat.
6. After preheating, place the sirloin roast into the Air Fryer Basket. Press "Start" to begin cooking.
7. While cooking, flip the sirloin roast once halfway through.
8. After cooking, remove the sirloin roast and place it on a platter for about 10 minutes.
9. Cut the beef roast into desired-sized slices and serve.

INGREDIENTS:

- Non-stick baking spray
- Smoked paprika – 15 g
- Ground cumin – 5 g
- Garlic powder – 5 g
- Salt and ground black pepper – as required
- Beef sirloin roast – 1100 g

Cook time: 20 minutes
Serves: 4

Per Serving:
Calories 450, Carbs 2.2g,
Fat 17.2g, Protein 66.7g

Herbed Beef Chuck Roast

INGREDIENTS:

- Beef chuck roast – 1 (900-g)
- Olive oil – 15 ml
- Dried rosemary – 2 g, crushed
- Dried thyme – 2 g, crushed
- Salt – as required
- Non-stick baking spray

Cook time: 45 minutes
Serves: 6

Per Serving:
Calories 304, Carbs 0.1g,
Fat 14g, Protein 41.5g

DIRECTIONS:

1. In a bowl, add the oil, herbs, and salt and blend to incorporate. Coat the beef roast with herb mixture generously. Grease the "Air Fryer Basket" with baking spray.
2. Select "Air Fry" and adjust the temperature to 185°C. Set the time for 45 minutes, press "Start" to preheat.
3. After preheating, place the beef roast into the Air Fryer Basket. Press "Start" to begin cooking.
4. While cooking, flip the beef roast once halfway through.
5. After cooking, remove the beef roast and place it onto a cutting board.
6. Cover the beef roast with foil for about 20 minutes before slicing.
7. Cut the beef roast into desired-size slices and serve.

Glazed Beef Short Ribs

DIRECTIONS:

1. Place the ribs and remaining ingredients into a resealable bag.
2. Seal the bag and shake to coat well. Refrigerate overnight.
3. Grease the "Air Fryer Basket" with baking spray.
4. Select "Air Fry" and then adjust the temperature to 195°C.
5. Set the time for 8 minutes and press "Start" to preheat.
6. After preheating, place the ribs into the Air Fryer Basket. Press "Start" to begin cooking.
7. While cooking, flip the ribs once halfway through.
8. After cooking, remove the ribs and enjoy right away.

INGREDIENTS:

- Bone-in beef short ribs – 1 kg
- Fresh ginger – 3 g, finely grated
- Balsamic vinegar – 60 ml
- Sugar – 10 g
- Green onions – 1, chopped
- Low-sodium soy sauce – 120 ml
- Sriracha – 5 ml
- Ground black pepper – as required
- Non-stick baking spray

Cook time: 8 minutes
Serves: 4

Per Serving:
Calories 496, Carbs 6.5g,
Fat 20.5g, Protein 67.6g

Crispy Sirloin Steaks

INGREDIENTS:

- All-purpose flour – 50 g
- Salt and ground black pepper – as required
- Eggs – 2
- Breadcrumbs – 115 g
- Sirloin steaks – 3, pounded
- Non-stick baking spray

Cook time: 14 minutes
Serves: 3

Per Serving:
Calories 540, Carbs 35.6g,
Fat 15.2g, Protein 61g

DIRECTIONS:

1. Place the flour, salt, and black pepper in a shallow bowl and blend to incorporate.
2. In a second shallow bowl, beat the eggs. In a third shallow bowl, place the breadcrumbs.
3. Coat the steak with flour, dip it into eggs, and coat it with panko.
4. Grease the "Air Fryer Basket" with baking spray.
5. Select "Air Fry" and adjust the temperature to 185°C. Set the time for 14 minutes, press "Start" to preheat.
6. After preheating, place the steaks into the Air Fryer Basket. Press "Start" to begin cooking.
7. While cooking, flip the steaks once halfway through.
8. After cooking, remove the steaks and enjoy right away.

Beef Casserole

DIRECTIONS:

1. Grease a baking pan with baking spray.
2. Add the beef and taco seasoning to a bowl and blend to incorporate.
3. Add the cheeses and salsa and stir to combine.
4. Place the mixture into the baking pan.
5. Select "Bake" and then adjust the temperature to 190°C.
6. Set the time for 25 minutes and press "Start" to preheat.
7. After preheating, place the baking pan into the Air Fryer Basket.
8. Press "Start" to begin cooking.
9. After cooking, remove the baking pan and enjoy moderately hot.

INGREDIENTS:

- Non-stick baking spray
- Ground beef – 900 g
- Taco seasoning – 20 g
- Cheddar cheese – 115 g, shredded
- Cottage cheese – 165 g
- Salsa – 260 g

Cook time: 25 minutes
Serves: 6

Per Serving:
Calories 412, Carbs 6.3g,
Fat 16.1g, Protein 56.4g

BBQ Pork Chops

INGREDIENTS:

- Pork loin chops – 6
- BBQ sauce – 115 g
- Salt and ground black pepper – as required
- Non-stick baking spray

Cook time: 15 minutes
Serves: 6

Per Serving:
Calories 757, Carbs 7.6g,
Fat 56.1g, Protein 51g

DIRECTIONS:

1. With a meat tenderizer, tenderize the chops completely.
2. Sprinkle the chops with a little salt and black pepper.
3. Add the BBQ and chops to a large bowl and blend to incorporate. Refrigerate, covered for about 6-8 hours.
4. Grease the "Air Fryer Basket" with baking spray.
5. Select "Bake" and adjust the temperature to 220°C. Set the time for 15 minutes, press "Start" to preheat.
6. After preheating, place the pork chops into the Air Fryer Basket. Press "Start" to begin cooking.
7. While cooking, flip the pork chops once halfway through.
8. After cooking, remove the pork chops and enjoy right away.

Spiced Pork Chops

DIRECTIONS:

1. In a large shallow bowl, mix the breadcrumbs and spices.
2. Coat the chops evenly with the breadcrumb mixture.
3. Grease the "Air Fryer Basket" with baking spray.
4. Select "Air Fry" and then adjust the temperature to 190°C.
5. Set the time for 17 minutes and press "Start" to preheat.
6. After preheating, place the pork chops into the Air Fryer Basket.
7. Press "Start" to begin cooking.
8. After 9 minutes of cooking, flip the pork chops.
9. After cooking, remove the pork chops and enjoy right away.

INGREDIENTS:

- Panko breadcrumbs – 75 g
- Paprika – 5 g
- Onion powder – 1¼ g
- Garlic powder – 1¼ g
- Salt and ground black pepper – as required
- Boneless pork chops – 2, trimmed
- Non-stick baking spray

Cook time: 17 minutes
Serves: 2

Per Serving:
Calories 305, Carbs 5.2g,
Fat 7g, Protein 38.1g

Rosemary Pork Loin

INGREDIENTS:

- Sugar – 30 g
- Dried rosemary – 10 g
- Garlic powder – 5 g
- Salt – as required
- Pork loin – 1 kg
- Non-stick baking spray

Cook time: 20 minutes
Serves: 6

Per Serving:
Calories 390, Carbs 6.1g,
Fat 21.1g, Protein 41.4g

DIRECTIONS:

1. Add the sugar, rosemary, garlic powder, and salt in a bowl and blend to incorporate.
2. Rub the pork loin with the rosemary mixture generously.
3. Grease the "Air Fryer Basket" with baking spray.
4. Select "Air Fry" and then adjust the temperature to 205°C.
5. Set the time for 20 minutes and press "Start" to preheat.
6. After preheating, place the pork loin into the Air Fryer Basket. Press "Start" to begin cooking.
7. While cooking, flip the pork loin once halfway through.
8. After cooking, remove the pork loin and place onto a cutting board. Cut into desired-sized slices and serve.

Caramelized Pork Shoulder

DIRECTIONS:

1. In a bowl, mix all ingredients except for pork shoulder.
2. Add the pork and coat with marinade generously.
3. Cover and refrigerate to marinate for about 2-8 hours.
4. Grease the "Air Fryer Basket" with baking spray.
5. Select "Air Fry" and then adjust the temperature to 180°C.
6. Set the time for 10 minutes and press "Start" to preheat.
7. After preheating, place the pork slice into the Air Fryer Basket.
8. Press "Start" to begin cooking.
9. After 10 minutes of cooking, adjust the temperature to 200°C for 7 minutes.
10. After cooking, remove the pork slice and enjoy right away.

INGREDIENTS:

- Low-sodium soy sauce – 45 ml
- Maple syrup – 10 g
- Sugar – 15 g
- Pork shoulder – 1 kg, trimmed and cut into slices
- Non-stick baking spray

Cook time: 17 minutes
Serves: 6

Per Serving:
Calories 464, Carbs 5.3g,
Fat 32.3g, Protein 31.1g

BBQ Pork Ribs

INGREDIENTS:

- Honey – 30 g, divided
- BBQ sauce 250 g
- 2 tablespoons tomato ketchup
- Worcestershire sauce – 15 ml
- Low-sodium soy sauce – 15 ml
- Garlic powder – 2½ g
- Ground white pepper – as required
- Pork ribs – 900 g
- Non-stick baking spray

Cook time: 13 minutes
Serves: 6

Per Serving:
Calories 490, Carbs 19.2g, Fat 26.9g, Protein 40.4g

DIRECTIONS:

1. Add all ingredients except pork ribs in a large bowl and blend to incorporate.
2. Add the pork ribs and coat with the mixture. Refrigerate to marinate for about 20 minutes.
3. Grease the "Air Fryer Basket" with baking spray.
4. Select "Air Fry" and then adjust the temperature to 180°C.
5. Set the time for 13 minutes and press "Start" to preheat.
6. After preheating, place the pork ribs into the Air Fryer Basket.
7. Press "Start" to begin, flip pork ribs once halfway through.
8. After cooking, remove the pork ribs and enjoy right away.

Seasoned Pork Tenderloin

DIRECTIONS:

1. Coat the pork tenderloin with oil and then rub it generously with barbecue rub.
2. Grease the "Air Fryer Basket" with baking spray.
3. Select "Bake" and then adjust the temperature to 175°C.
4. Set the time for 30 minutes and press "Start" to preheat.
5. After preheating, place the pork tenderloin into the Air Fryer Basket.
6. Press "Start" to begin cooking.
7. While cooking, flip the pork tenderloin once halfway through.
8. After cooking, remove the pork tenderloin and place it onto a cutting board.
9. Cover the pork tenderloin with a piece of foil for about 10 minutes.
10. Cut the pork tenderloin into desired-size slices and serve.

INGREDIENTS:

- Pork tenderloin – 900 g
- Olive oil – 30 ml, divided
- Barbecue seasoning rub – 30 g
- Non-stick baking spray

Cook time: 30 minutes
Serves: 6

Per Serving:
Calories 421, Carbs 2g,
Fat 25.1g, Protein 41.3g

Stuffed Pork Roll

INGREDIENTS:

- Green onion – 1, chopped
- Sun-dried tomatoes – 50 g, chopped finely
- Fresh parsley – 2 g, chopped
- Salt and ground black pepper
- Pork cutlets – 4, pounded slightly
- Paprika – 10 g
- Olive oil – 10 g
- Non-stick baking spray

Cook time: 15 minutes
Serves: 4

Per Serving:
Calories 244, Carbs 8.2g,
Fat 14.5g, Protein 20.1g

DIRECTIONS:

1. Mix the green onion, tomatoes, parsley, salt, and black pepper in a bowl.
2. Spread the tomato mixture over each pork cutlet. Roll each cutlet and secure it with cocktail sticks.
3. Rub the outer part of the rolls with paprika, salt, and black pepper. Coat the rolls with oil evenly.
4. Grease the "Air Fryer Basket" with baking spray. Select "Air Fry" and adjust the temperature to 200°C.
5. Set the time for 15 minutes and press "Start" to preheat.
6. After preheating, place the pork rolls into the Air Fryer Basket. Press "Start" to begin cooking.
7. While cooking, flip the pork rolls once halfway through. After cooking, enjoy right away.

Garlicky Lamb Chops

DIRECTIONS:

1. Mix the garlic, lemon juice, oil, Za'atar, salt, and black pepper in a large bowl.
2. Coat the chops with the garlic mixture. Grease the "Air Fryer Basket" with baking spray.
3. Select "Air Fry" and then adjust the temperature to 200°C.
4. Set the time for 15 minutes and press "Start" to preheat.
5. After preheating, place the chops into the Air Fryer Basket. Press "Start" to begin cooking.
6. While cooking, flip the chops once halfway through.
7. After cooking, remove the chops and enjoy right away.

INGREDIENTS:

- Non-stick baking spray
- Garlic cloves – 4, crushed
- Fresh lemon juice – 30 ml
- Olive oil – 5 ml
- Za'atar – 15 g
- Salt and ground black pepper
- Bone-in lamb loin chops – 8, trimmed

Cook time: 15 minutes
Serves: 4

Per Serving:
Calories 385, Carbs 1.1g,
Fat 15.8g, Protein 55.9g

Sweet & Sour Lamb Chops

INGREDIENTS:

- Lamb shoulder chops – 3
- Salt and ground black pepper – as required
- Sugar – 40 g
- Fresh lime juice – 30 ml
- Non-stick baking spray

Cook time: 40 minutes
Serves: 3

Per Serving:
Calories 405, Carbs 16.8g,
Fat 18.1g, Protein 44.2g

DIRECTIONS:

1. Season the lamb chops generously with salt and black pepper.
2. In a baking pan, place the chops and sprinkle with sugar, followed by the lime juice.
3. Grease the "Air Fryer Basket" with baking spray.
4. Select "Roast" and then adjust the temperature to 190°C.
5. Set the time for 40 minutes and press "Start" to preheat.
6. After preheating, place the chops into the Air Fryer Basket.
7. Press "Start" to begin cooking.
8. While cooking, flip the chops once halfway through.
9. After cooking, remove the chops and enjoy right away.

Almond Crusted Rack of Lamb

DIRECTIONS:

1. Season the rack of lamb with salt and black pepper evenly and then drizzle with cooking spray.
2. In a shallow dish, beat the egg. In another shallow dish, mix the breadcrumbs and almonds.
3. Dip the rack of lamb in egg and then coat with the almond mixture.
4. Grease the "Air Fryer Basket" with baking spray.
5. Select "Air Fry" and then adjust the temperature to 105°C.
6. Set the time for 30 minutes and press "Start" to preheat.
7. After preheating, place the rack of lamb into the Air Fryer Basket. Press "Start" to begin cooking.
8. After 30 minutes of cooking, adjust the temperature to 200°C for 5 minutes.
9. After cooking, remove the rack of lamb and place it onto a cutting board.
10. Cut the rack of lamb into individual chops and serve.

INGREDIENTS:

- Rack of lamb – 1
- Salt and ground black pepper – as required
- Egg – 1
- Breadcrumbs – 15 g
- Almonds – 85 g, chopped finely
- Non-stick baking spray

Cook time: 35 minutes
Serves: 6

Per Serving:
Calories 319, Carbs 3.9g,
Fat 19.6g, Protein 31g

Rosemary Leg of Lamb

INGREDIENTS:

- Bone-in leg of lamb – 900 g
- Olive oil – 30 ml
- Cayenne powder – 5 g
- Salt and ground black pepper – as required
- Fresh rosemary sprigs – 4
- Non-stick baking spray

Cook time: 1¼ hours
Serves: 4

Per Serving:
Calories 493, Carbs 2.1g,
Fat 24.1g, Protein 63.9g

DIRECTIONS:

1. Coat the leg of lamb with oil and sprinkle with cayenne powder, salt, and black pepper.
2. Wrap the leg of lamb with rosemary sprigs. Grease the "Air Fryer Basket" with baking spray.
3. Select "Air Fry" and then adjust the temperature to 150°C.
4. Set the time for 75 minutes and press "Start" to preheat.
5. After preheating, place the leg of lamb into an Air Fryer Basket. Press "Start" to begin cooking.
6. After cooking, remove the leg of lamb and place it onto a platter.
7. Cover the leg of lamb with a piece of foil for about 10 minutes.
8. Cut the leg of lamb into desired-sized pieces and serve.

Pork with Sweet Pepper

DIRECTIONS:

1. In a bowl, add the sweet peppers, onion, Herbs de Provence, salt, black pepper, and ½ tablespoon of oil and toss to coat well. Rub the pork pieces with mustard, salt, and black pepper.
2. Drizzle with the remaining oil.
3. In a baking dish, place the capsicum mixture and pork pieces and blend to incorporate.
4. Select "Air Fry" and adjust the temperature to 175 °C. Set the time for 16 minutes, press "Start" to preheat.
5. After preheating, place the baking pan into the Air Fryer Basket. Press "Start" to begin cooking.
6. While cooking, stir the pork mixture once halfway through.
7. After cooking, remove the baking pan and enjoy right away.

INGREDIENTS:

- Sweet peppers – 2, seeded and cut into thin strips
- Red onion – 1, thinly sliced
- Herbs de Provence – 10 g
- Salt and ground black pepper
- Olive oil – 15 ml, divided
- Pork loin – 350 g, trimmed and cut into 4 pieces
- Mustard – 10 g

Cook time: 16 minutes
Serves: 4

Per Serving:
Calories 267, Carbs 7g,
Fat 15.6g, Protein 24.1g

VEGETARIAN RECIPES

Potato au Gratin

INGREDIENTS:

- Non-stick baking spray
- Medium potatoes – 3 thinly sliced
- Garlic powder – 2½ g
- Salt and ground black pepper
- Heavy cream – 190 g
- Cheddar cheese – 360 g, shredded
- Unsalted butter – 15 g

Cook time: 20 minutes
Serves: 8

Per Serving:
Calories 294, Carbs 13.7g,
Fat 21.1g, Protein 12.9g

DIRECTIONS:

1. Grease a large, shallow baking pan with baking spray.
2. Arrange a layer of potato slices into the prepared baking pan.
3. Season the potato slices with garlic powder, salt and pepper.
4. Place a tablespoon of cream over potatoes, then top with a thin layer of cheese.
5. Repeat the process 4 times, overlapping slightly. Top with the butter into dots.
6. Select "Air Fry" and then adjust the temperature to 175°C.
7. Set the time for 20 minutes and press "Start" to preheat.
8. After preheating, place the baking pan into the Air Fryer Basket. Press "Start" to begin cooking.
9. After cooking, remove the baking pan and set aside for about 5 minutes before serving.

Courgette Gratin

DIRECTIONS:

1. Grease a baking pan with baking spray.
2. Place the heavy whipping cream, butter, and garlic powder in a microwave-safe dish and microwave for about 1 minute. Remove from the microwave and beat the mixture until smooth.
3. Arrange 1/3 of courgette and onion slices in the bottom of the prepared baking pan and sprinkle with some salt, black pepper, and 60 g of cheese.
4. Repeat the layers twice. Now, place the cream mixture on top evenly.
5. Select "Bake", adjust the temperature to 190°C. Set the time for 45 minutes and press "Start" to preheat.
6. After preheating, place the baking pan into the Air Fryer Basket. Press "Start" to begin cooking.
7. After cooking, remove the baking pan and set aside for about 5-10 minutes.

INGREDIENTS:

- Heavy whipping cream – 120 g
- Butter – 25 g
- Garlic powder – 2½ g
- Courgettes – 450 g, sliced
- Small onion – 1, thinly sliced
- Salt and ground black
- Cheese – 175 g, shredded

Cook time: 45 minutes
Serves: 8

Per Serving:
Calories 140, Carbs 3.9g,
Fat 11.8g, Protein 5.5g

Cheesy Spinach

INGREDIENTS:

- Non-stick baking spray
- Frozen spinach – 1 package, thawed
- Onion – 55 g, chopped
- Garlic cloves – 4, minced
- Cream cheese – 115 g, chopped
- Ground nutmeg – 2½ g
- Salt and ground black pepper – as required
- Parmesan cheese – 25 g, shredded

Cook time: 15 minutes
Serves: 3

Per Serving:
Calories 194, Carbs 7.3g,
Fat 15.5g, Protein 8.4g

DIRECTIONS:

1. Grease a baking pan with baking spray.
2. In a bowl, add spinach, onion, garlic, cream cheese, nutmeg, salt, and black pepper and blend to incorporate. Place the mixture into the baking pan.
3. Select "Air Fry" and then adjust the temperature to 175°C.
4. Set the time for 10 minutes and press "Start" to preheat.
5. After preheating, place the baking pan into the Air Fryer Basket. Press "Start" to begin cooking.
6. After 10 minutes of cooking, sprinkle the spinach mixture with Parmesan cheese.
7. After cooking, remove the baking pan and enjoy right away.

Parmesan Mixed Veggies

DIRECTIONS:

1. Grease a baking pan with baking spray.
2. Add all the ingredients except cheese and toss to coat well in a large bowl.
3. Select "Air Fry", adjust the temperature to 200°C. Set the time for 25 minutes, press "Start" to preheat.
4. After preheating, place the baking pan into the Air Fryer Basket. Press "Start" to begin cooking.
5. After 18 minutes of cooking, flip the vegetables and sprinkle with cheese evenly.
6. After cooking, remove the baking pan and enjoy right away.

INGREDIENTS:

- Olive oil – 15 ml
- Garlic cloves – 4, minced
- Cauliflower florets – 100 g
- Broccoli florets – 100 g
- Courgette – 115 g, sliced
- Fresh mushrooms – 110 g, sliced
- Sweet pepper – 2, sliced
- Balsamic vinegar – 50 ml
- Red pepper flakes – 5 g
- Salt and freshly ground black pepper
- Parmesan cheese – 30 g, grated

Cook time: 25 minutes
Serves: 5

Per Serving:
Calories 162, Carbs 20.1g,
Fat 6.1g, Protein 8.7g

Ratatouille

INGREDIENTS:

- Aubergine – 1, chopped
- Tomatoes – 3, chopped
- Garlic cloves – 3, minced
- Olive oil – 15 ml
- Balsamic vinegar – 15 ml
- Sweet pepper – 3, chopped
- Courgette – 1, chopped
- Small onions – 2, chopped
- Herbs de Provence – 30 g
- Salt and ground black

Cook time: 15 minutes
Serves: 4

Per Serving:
Calories 120, Carbs 21.3g,
Fat 4.6g, Protein 3.6g

DIRECTIONS:

1. Grease a baking pan with baking spray.
2. Add the vegetables, garlic, Herbs de Provence, oil, vinegar, salt, and black pepper in a large bowl and toss to coat well. Transfer the vegetable mixture to the prepared baking pan.
3. Select "Air Fry", adjust the temperature to 180°C. Set the time for 15 minutes and press "Start" to preheat.
4. After preheating, place the baking pan into the Air Fryer Basket. Press "Start" to begin cooking.
5. After cooking, remove the baking pan and serve.

Stuffed Sweet Peppers

DIRECTIONS:

1. Remove the tops of each sweet pepper and then discard the seeds. Finely chop the tops.
2. Put chopped sweet pepper tops, loaf, vegetables, garlic, parsley, salt, and black pepper into a bowl and blend to incorporate. Stuff each sweet pepper with the vegetable mixture.
3. Grease the "Air Fryer Basket" with baking spray. Select "Bake" and then adjust the temperature to 175°C.
4. Set the time for 60 minutes and press "Start" to preheat.
5. After preheating, place the capsicums into the Air Fryer Basket. Press "Start" to begin cooking.
6. After 50 minutes of cooking, top each sweet pepper with cheese. After cooking, remove them and serve.

INGREDIENTS:

- Sweet peppers – 6
- Bread roll – 1, finely chopped
- Carrot – 1, peeled and finely chopped
- Onion – 1, finely chopped
- Potato – 1, peeled and finely chopped
- Fresh green peas – 70 g, shelled
- Garlic cloves – 2, minced
- Fresh parsley – 5 g, chopped
- Cheddar cheese – 45 g, grated

Cook time: 1-hour
Serves: 6

Per Serving:
Calories 123, Carbs 21.7g,
Fat 2.7g, Protein 4.8g

Stuffed Aubergine

INGREDIENTS:

- Large aubergine – 2
- Olive oil – 20 ml, divided
- Fresh lemon juice – 20 ml, divided
- Cherry tomatoes – 16, quartered
- Tomato salsa – 70 g
- Fresh parsley – 2 g
- Salt and ground black pepper

Cook time: 25 minutes
Serves: 2

Per Serving:
Calories 192, Carbs 33.8g,
Fat 6.1g, Protein 6.9g

DIRECTIONS:

1. Grease the "Air Fryer Basket" with baking spray.
2. Select "Air Fry", adjust the temperature to 200°C. Set the timer for 15 minutes, press "Start" to preheat.
3. After preheating, place the aubergines into the Air Fryer Basket. Press "Start" to begin cooking.
4. After cooking, remove the aubergines, place them onto a platter. Cut each aubergine in half lengthwise.
5. Drizzle the halves with oil.
6. Again, grease the "Air Fryer Basket" with baking spray. Select "Air Fry", adjust the temperature to 180°C.
7. Set the time for 10 minutes and press "Start" to preheat.

8. After preheating, place the aubergine halves into the Air Fryer Basket.Press "Start" to begin cooking.
9. After cooking, remove the aubergine halves and set aside for about 5 minutes.
10.   Carefully scoop out the flesh, leaving about ¼-inch away from the edges. Drizzle with lemon juice.
11.   Transfer the aubergine flesh into a bowl. Add the tomatoes, salsa, parsley, salt, black pepper, remaining oil, and lemon juice and blend to incorporate. Stuff the haves with salsa mixture and serve.

Stuffed Courgette

INGREDIENTS:

- Medium courgettes – 4, halved
- Sweet pepper – 150 g, minced
- Olives – 90 g, pitted and minced
- Tomatoes – 100 g, minced
- Garlic cloves – 2, minced
- Dried oregano – 5 g, crushed
- Salt and ground black
- Feta cheese – 60 g, crumbled

Cook time: 20 minutes
Serves: 8

Per Serving:
Calories 59, Carbs 6.2g,
Fat 3.2g, Protein 2.9g

DIRECTIONS:

1. With a melon baller, scoop out the flesh of each courgette half. Discard the flesh.
2. In a bowl, add the sweet peppers, olives, tomatoes, garlic, oregano, salt, and black pepper and blend to incorporate. Stuff each courgette half evenly with the veggie mixture.
3. Grease the "Air Fryer Basket" with baking spray. Select "Bake" and then adjust the temperature to 175°C.
4. Set the time for 20 minutes, press "Start" to preheat. Place the courgette halves into the Air Fryer Basket.
5. Press "Start" to begin cooking. After 15 minutes of cooking, top each courgette half with feta cheese.
6. After cooking, remove the courgette halves and enjoy right away.

Tofu with Veggies

DIRECTIONS:

1. Grease a baking pan with baking spray.
2. Put tofu and remaining ingredients into a large-sized bowl and toss to incorporate. Place the tofu mixture into the baking pan.
3. Select "Air Fry", adjust the temperature to 200°C. Set the time for 15 minutes, press "Start" to preheat.
4. After preheating, place the baking pan into the Air Fryer Basket. Press "Start" to begin cooking.
5. While cooking, toss the tofu mixture once halfway through.
6. After cooking, remove the baking pan and sprinkle with sesame seeds. Enjoy right away.

INGREDIENTS:

- Firm tofu – 225 g, drained and cubed
- Broccoli florets – 135 g
- Sweet pepper – 1, seeded and sliced
- Vegetable oil – 30 ml
- Soy sauce – 30 ml
- Maple syrup – 20 g
- Salt and ground black pepper
- Sesame seeds – 10 g

Cook time: 15 minutes
Serves: 3

Per Serving:
Calories 201, Carbs 13.3g,
Fat 14g, Protein 9g

Veggie Rice

INGREDIENTS:

- Cooked white rice – 400 g
- Vegetable oil – 15 ml
- Sesame oil – 10 ml,
  Water – 15 ml
- Salt and ground white pepper
- Large egg – 1, lightly beaten
- Frozen green peas – 75 g,
  thawed
- Frozen carrots – 75 g, thawed
- Soy sauce – 5 ml
- Sriracha sauce – 5 ml

Cook time: 12 minutes
Serves: 5

Per Serving:
Calories 153, Carbs 4g,
Fat 8.2g, Protein 7.1g

DIRECTIONS:

1. Grease the baking pan with baking spray.
2. Add the rice, vegetable oil, one teaspoon of sesame oil, water, salt, and white pepper in a large bowl and blend to incorporate. Place the rice mixture into the baking pan.
3. Select "Air Fry", adjust the temperature to 195°C. Set the time for 18 minutes, press "Start" to preheat.
4. After preheating, place the baking pan into the Air Fryer Basket. Press "Start" to begin cooking.
5. After 6 minutes, stir the rice mixture once. After 12 minutes of cooking, place the beaten egg over the rice.

6. After 15 minutes of cooking, stir in the peas and carrots.
7. Meanwhile, in a bowl, mix soy sauce, Sriracha sauce, and the remaining sesame oil.
8. After cooking, remove the baking pan and transfer the rice mixture into a serving bowl.
9. Drizzle with the sauce and serve.

DESSERT RECIPES

Red Velvet Cupcakes

INGREDIENTS:

- Refined flour – 130 g
- Icing sugar – 50 g
- Beet powder – 5 g
- Cocoa powder – 2½ g
- Peanut butter – 120 g
- Small eggs – 2
- Unsalted butter – 115 g
- Cream cheese – 115 g, softened
- Powdered sugar – 260 g
- Vanilla extract – 5 ml
- Salt – ¾ g

Cook time: 12 minutes
Serves: 6

Per Serving:
Calories 563, Carbs 26g,
Fat 66g, Protein 8.9g

DIRECTIONS:

1. For cupcakes: in a bowl, add flour, icing sugar, beet powder, cocoa powder, peanut butter and eggs and with an electric mixer, whisk to incorporate thoroughly. Place the mixture into 6 silicon cups.
2. Select "Air Fry", adjust the temperature to 170°C. Set the time for 12 minutes and press "Start" to preheat.
3. After preheating, place the silicon cups into the Air Fryer Basket. Press "Start" to begin cooking.
4. After cooking, remove the silicon cups and place onto a wire rack to cool for around 10 minutes.
5. For frosting: in a large bowl, add butter, cream cheese, vanilla extract and salt and whisk to incorporate thoroughly. Add the powdered sugar, one cup at a time, whisking well after each addition.
6. Spread frosting evenly over each cupcake and serve.

Lemon Mousse

DIRECTIONS:

1. In a bowl, add all the ingredients and blend to incorporate. Transfer the mixture into 2 ramekins.
2. Select "Bake" and then adjust the temperature to 175°C.
3. Set the time for 12 minutes and press "Start" to preheat.
4. After preheating, place the ramekins into the Air Fryer Basket. Press "Start" to begin cooking.
5. After cooking, remove the ramekins and place them onto a wire rack to cool.
6. Refrigerate for at least 3 hours before serving.

INGREDIENTS:

- Cream cheese – 115 g, softened
- Heavy cream – 120 g
- Fresh lemon juice – 30 ml
- Liquid stevia – 4-6 drops

Cook time: 12 minutes
Serves: 2

Per Serving:
Calories 305, Carbs 2.7g,
Fat 31g, Protein 5g

Vanilla Crème Brûlée

INGREDIENTS:

- Non-stick baking spray
- Egg yolks – 6
- White sugar – 150 g, divided
- Salt – 1 pinch
- Heavy whipping cream –500g
- Vanilla extract – 10 ml

Cook time: 32 minutes
Serves: 6

Per Serving:
Calories 290, Carbs 26.9g,
Fat 19.3g, Protein 3.5g

DIRECTIONS:

1. Add the egg yolks, 50 g of sugar, and salt in a bowl and beat until well combined.
2. Add whipping cream and vanilla extract and whisk until well blended. Divide the mixture into 6 ramekins.
3. With a piece of foil, cover each ramekin tightly.
4. Select "Air Fry", adjust the temperature to 185°C. Set the time for 32 minutes and press "Start" to preheat.
5. After preheating, place the ramekins into the Air Fryer Basket. Press "Start" to begin cooking.
6. After cooking, remove the ramekins and place them onto a rack.
7. Carefully remove the foil from each ramekin and let them cool completely.
8. With plastic wrap, cover each ramekin and refrigerate for 1 hour.
9. Remove the plastic wrap before serving, and sprinkle the ramekins with the remaining sugar evenly.

Banana Mug Cake

DIRECTIONS:

1. Lightly grease 2 ramekins with baking spray. Mix the flour, baking soda, cinnamon, and salt in a bowl.
2. In another bowl, add the mashed banana and sugar and beat well.
3. Add the butter, the egg yolk, and the vanilla and blend to incorporate.
4. Add the flour mixture and mix until just combined. Place the mixture into the ramekins.
5. Select "Bake", adjust the temperature to 175°C. Set the time for 30 minutes and press "Start" to preheat.
6. After preheating, place the ramekins into the Air Fryer Basket. Press "Start" to begin cooking.
7. After cooking, remove the ramekins and place them onto a wire rack to cool slightly before serving.

INGREDIENTS:

- Non-stick baking spray
- All-purpose flour – 70 g
- Ground cinnamon – 1¼ g
- Baking soda – 2 g
- Salt – 1¼ g
- Banana – 225 g, peeled and mashed
- Sugar – 25 g
- Butter – 30 g, melted
- Egg yolks – 2
- Vanilla extract – 2½ ml

Cook time: 30 minutes
Serves: 2

Per Serving:
Calories 430, Carbs 6.9g,
Fat 16.6g, Protein 66g

Apple Doughnuts

INGREDIENTS:

- Apple cider – 240 ml
- All-purpose flour – 340 g
- Baking powder – 4 g
- Baking soda – 2 g
- Ground cinnamon– 2½ g
- Salt – 1¼ g
- Brown sugar – 85 g
- Unsalted butter – 30 g, softened
- Egg 1
- Pink lady apple – ½, peeled, cored and grated
- Non-stick baking spray

Cook time: 30 minutes
Serves: 6

Per Serving:
Calories 327, Carbs 63.1g,
Fat 5.2g, Protein 6.9g

DIRECTIONS:

1. In a medium saucepan, add the apple cider over medium-high heat and bring it to a boil.
2. Now, adjust the heat to low and simmer for about 15 minutes or until the cider reduces to ¼ cup.
3. Remove the pan from heat and transfer the apple cider into a bowl. Refrigerate to cool.
4. In a large bowl, add flour, baking powder, baking soda, cinnamon, and salt and blend to incorporate.
5. Add the brown sugar and butter to another bowl, and with an electric hand mixer, whisk until light and fluffy.
6. Add the egg and whisk well.
7. Add the cooled apple cider and blend to incorporate.
8. Add the flour mixture and

blend to incorporate.

9. Add the grated apple and mix until a dough forms.

10. Now, place the dough onto a lightly floured surface, and with your hands, knead until a soft dough comes together.

11. With plastic wrap, wrap the dough and refrigerate for about 30 minutes.

12. Now, roll the dough onto a lightly floured surface to a 1-inch thickness.

13. With a 3-inch doughnut cutter, cut the doughnuts.

14. Grease the "Air Fryer Basket" with baking spray.

15. Select "Air Fry" and then adjust the temperature to 185°C.

16. Set the time for 2 minutes and press "Start" to preheat.

17. After 2 minutes, turn off the unit.

18. Immediately arrange the doughnuts into "Air Fryer Basket".

19. Slide the basket inside and let the dough rest in the turned-off Air Fryer for about 5 minutes.

20. After 5 minutes, adjust the temperature to 185°C.

21. Set the time for 5 minutes and press "Start" to begin cooking.

22. After 3 minutes of cooking, flip the doughnuts.

23. After cooking, remove the doughnuts and place them onto a platter.

24. Serve warm.

Lava Cake

INGREDIENTS:

- All-purpose flour – 50 g
- Chocolate chips – 110 g
- Unsalted butter – 120 g, softened
- Large eggs – 2, Large egg yolks – 2
- Confectioners' sugar – 130 g
- Peppermint extract – 5 ml
- Powdered sugar – 15 g

Cook time: 10 minutes
Serves: 2

Per Serving:
Calories 262, Carbs 3.6g,
Fat 26.1g, Protein 7.6g

DIRECTIONS:

1. Grease 4 ramekins with baking spray, then dust each with a little flour.
2. In a microwave-safe bowl, place the chocolate chips and butter and microwave on high heat for about 30 seconds. Remove the bowl from the microwave and stir the mixture well.
3. Add the eggs, egg yolks, and confectioners' sugar and whisk until well combined.
4. Add the flour and peppermint extract and gently stir to combine.
5. Place the mixture into the prepared ramekins evenly.
6. Select "Air Fry", adjust the temperature to 190°C. Set the time for 12 minutes, press "Start" to preheat.
7. After preheating, place the ramekins into the Air Fryer Basket. Press "Start" to begin cooking.
8. After cooking, remove the ramekins and place them onto a wire rack for about 5 minutes.

Chocolate Loaf Cake

DIRECTIONS:

1. Grease a loaf pan with baking spray. Mix the flour, cocoa powder, sugar, baking soda, baking powder, and salt in a bowl.
2. Add the egg, applesauce, yogurt, and vanilla extract to another bowl. Beat until well combined.
3. Then, add in the flour mixture and mix until just combined. Add the peanut butter and mix until smooth.
4. Gently fold in the chocolate chips. Place the mixture into the prepared pan.
5. Select "Air Fry", adjust the temperature to 175°C. Set the time for 30 minutes, press "Start" to preheat.
6. After preheating, place the loaf pan into the Air Fryer Basket. Press "Start" to begin cooking.
7. After cooking, remove the loaf pan and place it onto a wire rack for 10-15 minutes.
8. Cut the cake into desired-sized slices and serve.

INGREDIENTS:

- All-purpose flour – 100 g
- Cocoa powder – 30 g
- White sugar – 50 g
- Baking soda – 2 g
- Baking powder – 2 g
- Salt – ¾ g,
- Egg – 1
- Unsweetened applesauce – 55 g
- Plain Greek yogurt – 65 g
- Vanilla extract – 2½ ml
- Creamy peanut butter – 120 g
- Mini chocolate chips – 60 g

Cook time: 30 minutes
Serves: 8

Per Serving:
Calories 191, Carbs 24.9g,
Fat 8.6g, Protein 6.1g

Apple Crisp

INGREDIENTS:

- Non-stick baking spray
- Apple – 260 g, peeled, cored and sliced
- Sugar – 50 g, divided
- Cornstarch – 10 g
- All-purpose flour – 25 g
- Ground cinnamon – 1¼ g
- Salt – 1 pinch
- Cold butter – 20 g, chopped
- Rolled oats – 20 g

Cook time: 40 minutes
Serves: 2

Per Serving:
Calories 337, Carbs 64.3g, Fat 9.6g, Protein 2.8g

DIRECTIONS:

1. Lightly grease 2 ramekins with baking spray.
2. Place apple slices, 1 teaspoon of sugar, and cornstarch in a bowl and toss to coat well.
3. Divide the plum mixture into the ramekins.
4. Mix the flour, remaining sugar, cinnamon, and salt in a bowl.
5. With 2 forks, blend in the butter until a crumbly mixture forms.
6. Add the oats and gently stir to combine.
7. Place the oat mixture over apple slices into each ramekin.
8. Select "Bake" and then adjust the temperature to 175°C.
9. Set the time for 40 minutes and press "Start" to preheat.

Notes

.

10. After preheating, place the
    ramekins into the Air Fryer Basket.
11. Press "Start" to begin cooking.
12. After cooking, remove the
    ramekins and place them onto a wire rack to cool for about
    10 minutes before serving.

Cherry Clafoutis

INGREDIENTS:

- Fresh cherries – 335 g, pitted
- Vodka – 45 ml
- All-purpose flour – 40 g
- White sugar – 25 g
- Salt – 1 pinch, Powdered sugar – 35 g
- Sour cream – 125 g
- Egg – 1, Butter 15 g

Cook time: 25 minutes
Serves: 4

Per Serving:
Calories 241, Carbs 29g,
Fat 10.1g, Protein 3.9g

DIRECTIONS:

1. Grease a cake pan with baking spray. In a bowl, mix the cherries and vodka.
2. In another bowl, mix the flour, sugar, and salt. Add the sour cream and egg, and mix until a smooth dough forms. Place the flour mixture into the prepared cake pan.
3. Spread the cherry mixture on top of the flour mixture evenly.
4. Select "Air Fry", adjust the temperature to 180°C. Set the time for 25 minutes, press "Start" to preheat.
5. After preheating, place the cake pan into the Air Fryer Basket. Press "Start" to begin cooking.
6. After cooking, remove the cake pan onto a wire rack to cool for about 10 minutes.

Cranberry Muffins

DIRECTIONS:

1. Add the almond milk, eggs, and vanilla extract to a blender and pulse for about 20-30 seconds.
2. Add the flour, sugar, baking powder, cinnamon, and salt and pulse for 30-45 seconds until well blended.
3. Transfer the mixture to a bowl. Gently fold in half of the cranberries and walnuts.
4. Place the mixture into 8 silicone muffin cups and top each with the remaining cranberries.
5. Select "Air Fry", adjust the temperature to 165°C. Set the time for 15 minutes and press "Start" to preheat.
6. After preheating, place the muffin cups into the Air Fryer Basket.
7. Press "Start" to begin cooking. After cooking, remove the muffin cups and enjoy once they have cooled.

INGREDIENTS:

- Unsweetened almond milk – 65 ml
- Large eggs – 2
- Vanilla extract – 2½ ml
- Flour – 150 g, Sugar – 50 g
- Baking powder – 4 g
- Ground cinnamon – 1¼ g
- Salt – ¾ g
- Fresh cranberries – 50 g
- Walnuts – 25 g, chopped

Cook time: 15 minutes
Serves: 8

Per Serving:
Calories 102, Carbs 9g,
Fat 6.3g, Protein 3.7g

CONCLUSION

The air fryer has revolutionized cooking by offering a healthier alternative to traditional frying methods without sacrificing flavor or texture. Its journey from an idea to a kitchen staple reflects the continuous innovation in the culinary world. Reduced oil consumption, efficient cooking times, and easy cleanup have made air fryers a game-changer for health-conscious individuals and busy households.

Efficient and safe air frying is a skill that develops with practice. Preheating, avoiding overcrowding, flipping or shaking, and experimenting with seasonings are crucial steps toward mastering the art of air frying. Keeping an eye on cooking times, checking for doneness, and prioritizing safety ensure delicious and safe culinary creations. Don't be afraid to try new recipes, tweak cooking times, or play with seasonings to suit your taste.

NOTES

Printed in Great Britain
by Amazon